Y2K...

CRYING WOLF or WORLD CRISIS?

Y2K...
Crying Wolf or World Crisis?

By

James F. Gauss, PhD.

"I have told you these things, so that in me you may have peace. In this world you will have trouble. But take heart! I have overcome the world."

(John 16:33)

Bridge-Logos *Publishers*
North Brunswick, NJ

Unless otherwise indicated, the Scripture quotations in this publication are from the Holy Bible: New International Version. Copyright © 1973, 1978, 1984 by the International Bible Society. Used by permission of Zondervan Bible Publishers.

Y2K: Crying Wolf or World Crisis?

Library of Congress Catalog Card Number: 98-74415
International Standard Book Number:0-88270-760-4

Published by:

Bridge-Logos *Publishers*
1300 Airport Road, Suite E
North Brunswick, NJ 08902

Disclaimer

The entire contents of this book is intended for informational purposes only in regard to the subject matter being covered. It is provided with the understanding by the reader that neither the author nor the publisher is engaged in, nor offering any legal, medical, financial, or other professional services through this publication. The reader bears all the risk relating to the use of any of this information, which is provided without any warranty or indemnity of any kind. None of the information within this publication should be used as a substitute for any form of professional advice or service where such may be required or beneficial.

Contents

Preface ... ix
1.Catching and Incubating the "Bug" ... 1
2.How Will It Affect Us? ... 5
3.A General Overview of Bugdom ... 9
4.Business (Not) as Usual ... 13
5.It's the Economy! ... 21
6.Out Go the Lights ... 29
7.Government Malfeasance ... 33
8.Defend Me Not ... 45
9.Triage or Flat Line? ... 51
10.Hello? Anybody Out There? ... 57
11.Honk! Honk! But Nowhere To Go ... 61
12.The World's Cure ... 65
13.But Seek First … ... 73
14.If My People 79
15.Building Your Hedge ... 87
16.Staying In Control (The Caleb Principle) ... 95
17.Equipping The Saints ... 101
18.The Harvest Is Ripe ... 109
19.Seek, And You Will Find ... 115

20.Give Your PC The Boot (Up) 125
21.Keeping The Gates Open 137
22.A Penny Saved … 143
23.No Place Like Home 153
24.It's A Community Thing 187
Epilogue 193
Addendum 1 197
Addendum 2 205
Addendum 3 211
Addendum 4 217
Addendum 5 221
Addendum 6 223
Addendum 7 227
Bibliography 251
Index 257
Biography of Dr. James Gauss 277

Dedication

To my best friend, wife, and companion for life, Kathleen,
for all her encouragement and support;
to our beloved adult children: Deb, James, Teresa, and Jeff;
to our dear Tina whom we miss so much;
and to our beautiful grandchildren: Jason, Scottie, and Trina.
May God richly bless you.

Preface

Could it really happen? Could the most anticipated New Year's Eve party in our lifetimes really usher in a digital nightmare when our wired-up-the-wazoo civilization grinds to a halt?

"The Day the World Shuts Down" *Newsweek*, June 2, 1997

It's Friday night, December 31, 1999, and you, like the majority of global citizens are caught up in the uniqueness and celebration of welcoming in a new millennium. No big deal, you might think. Your grandparents and great grand-parents witnessed turning the corner into the twentieth century that ushered in a rapid acceleration of the industrial revolution. It brought you all the conveniences you enjoy now. It is hard for you to imagine what you would do without all your electronic gadgets and wizardry.

As you celebrate the evening with family and friends, you find your thoughts drifting on occasion to things you have heard over the past few months. Will Christ return soon, as some have predicted or hoped? Will the year 2000 and the century to follow ring in unimaginable advances and prosperity for mankind? Is this Year 2000 crisis you've heard so much about in the last couple of months for real? With so much excitement around you, the thoughts quickly pass and you join in once again in the New Year's Eve merriment.

It's now 10:59 (CST) that evening, and as your family tradition has been, you all gather around the television to watch the ball drop at Times Square in New York City. As the clock nears twelve midnight in New York, you chant along with the Times Square crowd of thousands: "Five, four, three, two, one . . ." Your television screen suddenly becomes snowy—the way you have experienced a dozen times before during stormy weather—as if the signal has been lost. Nobody appears to be there—no picture, no sound other than the snowy buzz and crackle. Is something interrupting your reception? You quickly channel surf to other stations. Nothing but snow! Everyone void of Times Square hoopla! Except for stations originating outside the Eastern time zone. Some of those stations are reporting excitedly about the confusion coming out of New York City and elsewhere on the east coast. But you are not quite grasping it all—you are still focused on your own celebration at home in the upper Midwest, an hour behind New York.

Then, like an intestinal flu, you get this strong queasy feeling in the pit of your stomach: Did the "Bug" hit New York City? You're trying to fix snacks for your guests, but you can't concentrate. You can't resist your impulses any longer. It's 11:15 your time, and you flip on the radio, tuning in for any news. Your fear is quickly confirmed. Much of the eastern seaboard is in a blackout. Transportation is at a standstill, elevators have stalled, telecommunication is spotty, at best, and some people are in total panic trying to get home.

"Can this be for real?" you think.

The ache in the pit of your stomach gets worse, and beads of sweat emerge on your forehead. By now your guests are also expressing some concern, but try to dismiss any consequences of the Bug laughingly. Instead, most try to stay tuned into their local celebration of welcoming the year 2000. You try to be a gracious host, but your thoughts keep wandering as your anxiety grows. It is now 11:59.

It's ten below outside right now, but you were thoughtful and enhanced the warmth and coziness of the family room with the simulated wood burning of your gas fireplace. Everyone prepares for the final countdown with whistles, horns, pots and pans poised for a noisy welcome. Even your young children and those of your friends have been included for this very special, once-in-a-lifetime shindig. Someone's been designated the official timekeeper as the last minute of 1999 ticks by: "Nine, eight, seven," everyone begins to shout. "Six, five, four . . ."

Your anticipation and excitement is tempered by the increasing queasiness you feel. "Three, two, one . . ."

Blackness! Even your gas fireplace is starting to flicker and sputter. Someone goes to the front door to look outside. No street lights and few vehicles on the street. You grope for some candles and matches. You light several candles and ask your guests to place them around, and reach for the phone to dial the utility company. No dial tone. You click several times, but nothing. Total silence.

It is now thirty minutes past midnight, and you have noticed that it seems a little bit cooler in the house. You check the thermostat. It is set at "70", but the thermometer reads "62." You have your spouse check the furnace. It's not running. The hot water heater is also out.

Your nervous guests decide they better start heading home. Within minutes some return inside, out of the howling January wind. Their cars will not start. The ignition switches do not even make a sound. It looks like you might have some unexpected overnight guests.

You and a few others stay up through the dark night waiting for the utility company to restore power. But no power comes. The house gets colder, and you and your guests become increasingly uncomfortable.

"What is going on?" you wonder.

No, this isn't some Sci-fi scenario, or horror flick. You haven't been dropped into an old Rod Serling "Twilight Zone." You have caught the "Bug." You and all your guests and neighbors. What bug? Is it Asian? Brazilian? European? American? No, it is universal. It is the *Millennial Bug*. The Year 2000 computer glitch—also known as Y2K—you have heard so much about, but dismissed without interest because you were occupied with what you thought were more important matters.

Does the preceding drama sound far-fetched? Let us all pray and hope so. For most it is unthinkable. For some it is not only plausible, but it is potential reality. However, despite the thousands of articles written, programs aired, and warnings given throughout the industrialized world, the majority of people seem oblivious to the problem and the potential impact it will have on their life come January 1, 2000—and especially January 3, 2000, when millions go back to work that Monday.

The irony of it all is that the technology of the latter part of the twentieth century that was heralded as ushering in the era of wealth, short work weeks, and abundant leisure, is the same technology that is likely to humble the world on January 1, 2000. In the 1950s and 1960s, the invention of the computer—then behemoths that filled entire rooms—were envisioned as a technological innovation of man's infinite genius that would propel him to greatness beyond what he could ever imagine. This innovation of his cunning would bring ease and leisure to every area of his life and provide him with ultimate control of everything. And therein lies the problem.

Computers—from supercomputer mainframes to personal computers—and the mini-computer-like microprocessors have invaded every aspect of our life: from bill processing and record-keeping, to metered utilities and gas pumps, to electronic gadgets and wizardry, to banking and financial records, to the vehicles we drive and the equipment we use. The list is pervasive and endless. It is a technology that is intertwined throughout the globe: under the sea, under and across the nations of the world, through the air, and in the outer space above us.

This book is not meant to be an authoritative end-all book on the subject of the Year 2000. Rather it is meant to alert Christians and others of the nature and depth of the problem we will all confront, to help everyone gain a clearer understanding of how this could potentially affect their daily life, to provide some practical guidance, and to point all readers to the foundation on which they should stand and rely: Jesus Christ, Lord and Savior of all who will seek and call upon him. I encourage you to seek out other sources of Year 2000 information, as well as stay informed through current updates on the issue. You should also get involved with your church and community in addressing Y2K issues and helping your church and community become adequately prepared.

It is my hope that you will prayerfully and thoughtfully read the contents of this book and reflect on your preparedness to enter the year 2000—rationally and spiritually.

Jim Gauss

1

Catching and Incubating the "Bug"

. . . the ultimate indignity: the world laid low by two lousy digits.

"The Day the World Shuts Down"
Newsweek, June 2, 1997

It is, perhaps, difficult for the majority of people—busy with careers, raising families, and a multitude of other worthy endeavors—to comprehend how two little numbers; two lousy digits can be creating such a ruckus throughout the world. What exactly is the *Millennium Bug* (also known as Year 2000, or Y2K), you might ask, and how did we get it? The bug itself is actually quite simple in origin. What is difficult for many to understand is how we could have been put so effectively at its mercy. Particularly when people, supposedly much smarter than ourselves, spurred us on into the technological era of microwaves, cell phones, high resolution TV, electronic mail, and the like. How could they have put us into such a vulnerable predicament?

In a way we are all responsible for this dilemma. We have become a country and a world that craves fast living, short-cuts, and quick fixes. So did computer programmers during the decades of the 1950s through the 1980s. Before the microchip of today that can store more than could a whole room full of Univacs in the 1950s, programmers were desperate for computer memory. Since it was a well accepted practice here and abroad to abbreviate dates into two digits, so that October 23, 1958 became 10/23/58, two digits, "1" and "9" could be lopped off each year and save thousands of bits of memory. This became a universally accepted practice throughout the rapidly moving computerized world. Many computer programmers of the era who worked with now ancient computer languages (like COBOL) became very creative, using their own code words for dates. While common COBOL was only one of hundreds of computer languages used, the rest some experts say "*is a Tower of Babel*" (1). Although some software exists to help with the decoding process with some languages, many are in embedded (hidden) systems and machinery, often not readily accessible, and must be painstakingly hunted down and decoded manually.

What is amazing about this whole thing, is that among the thousands of computer whizzes and high tech professionals out there, no one apparently had the vision to see the problems these two practices would cause in the not-to-distant future. In all fairness though, many programmers assumed that the systems they designed and programmed would be upgraded or junked by now. With a great number of older mainframes, their older personal computer cousins, and their accompanying outdated software around the world that read a four digit year as only the last two numbers (so that 1998 becomes 98), the scenario for a computer brouhaha was created. So, when 1999 turns into 2000, a lot of computers, if not re-coded, will see a big 00, and likely read the year as 1900. To make matters even more challenging for today's Year 2000 fix-it programmers, date codes can show up as frequently as every 50 lines of code (2). That is problematic enough, but when you do not know what code or codes those imaginative programmers of yesterday used to designate dates, the task becomes even more daunting.

How will computers, electronic equipment, and machinery with embedded systems react if they cannot read 00 as the year 2000 come January 1, 2000? Many fear a combination of technological disasters: the equipment involved comes to an instantaneous halt and freezes up; or it scrambles data or destroys records; or it goes haywire, metering out incorrect information that cause chaos with other integrated systems or machinery. In any event, the scenarios are not pretty or comfortable to think about if a significant number of the country's critical systems are not ready to deal with the year 2000 in an effective and smooth manner. *"If we don't swat the millennium Bug* [by December 31, 1999] *we'll have troubles everywhere"*(2).

So, just how long have we known about the potential Year 2000 date glitch in the United States? With all the recent media hype you would think the big discovery was in 1997 or 1998. No, some branches of the federal government, as well as segments of the computer industry, have probably known about it for 30 years. That's right, *30 years!* According to 78-year old retired (now un-retired) Bob Bemer—one of the computer industry's acclaimed pioneers who invented and developed some of the earliest computer codes and operating systems—he tried to bring the problem to the attention of the federal government as early as 1969, but was rebuffed. It has been widely reported that in June, 1986, a South African computer programmer, Chris Anderson, ran an ad in the magazine *Computing SA*, claiming IBM's mainframes had a serious date *"time bomb."* IBM quickly threatened action against Mr. Anderson if the ad was not withdrawn. By the mid-1980s, a number of computer scientists, most notably world recognized Canadian computer consultant, Peter de Jager, were warning governments and businesses of the latent threat of Y2K. In 1989, the Social Security Administration inadvertently stumbled on the Year 2000 problem when a worker tried entering information that went beyond 1999 and the computer crashed. While this alerted SSA officials to their own potential Year 2000 problem, they apparently did not share that concern with other government agencies.

On July 15, 1996, President Clinton signed an Executive Order to set up the Presidential Commission on Critical Infrastructure Protection, which might lead some to believe he knew something was in the wind. But it was not until February 4, 1998 that President Clinton signed the first Executive Order that recognized the Year 2000 problem. This E.O. established a White House Council to coordinate the government's Year 2000 problem-solving effort. Two years earlier, however, there was movement on Capitol Hill with a subcommittee headed by Rep. Stephen Horn (R-Calif.) to study the potential impact of Y2K on the nation.

With all this early warning, why are we so ill prepared as a nation and the public so uninformed? We can only speculate on the possible answers to those questions.

2

How Will It Affect Us?

Could the most anticipated New Year's Eve party in our lifetimes really usher in a digital nightmare . . . ? Incredibly, according to computer experts, corporate information officers, congressional leaders and basically anyone who's given the matter a fair hearing, the answer is yes, yes, 2,000 times yes! (1)

Although this is obviously not the first time that mankind has entered into a new millennium (a period of one thousand years), it is the first time in which virtually the entire planet is linked by computers and computerized processes. In that sense, we are indeed a one world government and people. It no longer takes weeks to send vital information around the world, it takes only a fraction of a second. While a millennium is defined as an "*imagined golden age, a period of great happiness, peace, prosperity, etc.*" (2), this millennium appears to be destined for a rocky start according to the overwhelming majority of officials who are in the know about this issue.

There is widespread agreement across the nations of the world—from computer experts, corporate information officers, technocrats, economists, world leaders, and others informed on the nature of the crisis—that no matter what transpires in terms of fixing the problem before December 31, 1999, virtually every person in the world relying on modern conveniences will experience some disruption and uncertainty. The mind-boggling enormity of the Bug's influence worldwide is beyond the comprehension of most world citizens. "*Virtually every government, state and municipality,* a Newsweek article states, *as well as every large, midsize and small business in the world, is going to have to deal with this—in fact, if they haven't started already* [June, 1997] *it's just about too late"* (1).

It is this vastness and intricacy of the world of billions of "bugs" waiting to react to a digital change from 1999 to 2000 that has the world's computer experts, economists, and politicians nervously sitting on the edge of their seats. The task is so enormous and complex it is without question that the successful completion of the worldwide effort will not be finished until years after the year 2000 has come and gone. Peter de Jager, a highly sought after Canadian computer consultant, who has been sounding the Year 2000 alarm since the mid-1980s, is concerned that too many are not taking the problem serious enough, or spending sufficient money to rectify all the glitches. *"We know three things,* he says, *Many computer codes around the world are flawed. We have a deadline that can't be pushed back. And computer programmers are notorious for never finishing a project on time"* (3).

Another thing is also clear: a large number of U.S. governments—local, state, and federal—and their various agencies and departments; large corporations and small businesses; utility companies, and other vital services, are running behind schedule—some are just starting to assess the problem. Assessment is just the first step in dealing with the Year 2000 problem. Once a complete assessment of all systems and equipment that could be affected is completed, then a plan of action must be developed, adequately funded, and the needed personnel recruited. The problem is so massive and drudgingly detailed, that there are too few qualified computer specialists to tackle the job. It has been estimated that 350,000 jobs for computer scientists and programmers will go unfilled in the United States alone (4, 5).

If a company or organization is fortunate enough to have the necessary trained people in place, the laborious manual task of re-coding affected computer systems can begin. But computers are not the only things that need to be checked out. There may be billions of embedded time-stamped or silicone microprocessors in everything from coffee makers, photocopiers, elevators, machinery, and office equipment that need to be inspected and potentially replaced or scraped. It is a job that can take months or years depending on the size and complexity of an organization's computer system, equipment, or machinery.

Once re-coding is completed and microchips replaced, then the tedious job of system-wide testing, trouble-shooting, and re-testing begins and continues until everything works as hoped for. For larger companies, governments, and organizations, this testing will likely require integrated testing with systems in other departments, companies, etc., throughout the state, country, or worldwide. It is such a mammoth undertaking that large groups will need up to a year or more to work out all the bugs and glitches.

In addition, there are formidable obstacles for those that are trying to bring their systems into compliance with the Year 2000 date change. Time has already run out for on-time task completion for many companies, service sector organizations, and various departments and services of city, state, and federal governments due to a late start on fixing the problem. Many are still mistakenly thinking they have until December 31, 1999 to complete their mission. But with many companies and states operating on a fiscal year that starts July 1, their Year 2000 starts July 1, 1999. With insufficient resources of moneys and personnel, coupled with too little time, the stage for a potential disruption in our economy and lifestyle exists. "*If you're not changing code by November of this year* [1997], Peter de Jager warned, *you will not get this thing done on time—it's that simple*" (1).

Points to Ponder

1. What everyday conveniences do you take for granted that are operated by computers, electronics controlled by unseen microprocessors, or electricity?

2. Of these, which ones could you live without and still be comfortable? Still make a living?
3. When was the last time you went camping and really "roughed" it?
4. Can you name ten things that are vital to your daily needs that are controlled or would not function without computers or microprocessors?
5. At work, who is the person responsible for coordinating your company's or organization's Year 2000 project? Who is coordinating the effort for your community?

NEWS FLASH! July 14, 1998. *The tricky part of the White House's Y2K political problem will be telling everyone there's no need to stockpile canned food—while being alarmist enough to prod business leaders into action.*

TIME Daily

3

A General Overview of Bugdom

Fixing the Year 2000 problem is akin to taking apart the space shuttle, piece by piece, finding and fixing an unknown number of problems, then reassembling the vehicle, TESTING and RETESTING it, and hoping it will fly (1).

Vincent Mullineaux
President, Millennia III

Make no mistake about it, correcting the Y2K Bug is the biggest technological undertaking the world has ever seen. To underestimate or under prepare for the worldwide impact would be foolhardy and disastrous. Everyone who relies on some form of technology will be affected—some more, some less. Of great concern, although much of America's industry and government got a late start on addressing the problem, the United States is head and shoulders ahead of the rest of the world. "That's great!" you might think, until you realize how far away the U.S. as a whole is from the finish line. It is like running the mile and coming to the "bell lap" realizing that you have to run a five second lap to beat your best time. It can't be done, but you want to finish the race with the best time your weary legs can muster. It is also not a reason for euphoria, because we are reliant on a multitude of nations for commerce, military surveillance, telecommunication, energy supply, currency exchange, international loans and investments, world banking, etc.

As far ahead of other nations as the U.S. is, though lagging considerably behind an immovable deadline, key world nations are barely in the race. While Britain has made some strides forward, continental Europe, preoccupied with economic woes and establishing the Eurodollar, is lagging far behind and is very unlikely to be Y2K compliant in most areas (2). Japan, mired in political complacency on the issue and in deep financial trouble has had scant time and resources to devote to the problem. Other Asian and Southeast Asian countries, also in financial turmoil have barely, if at all, begun to address the problem. In Russia, itself in economic collapse, the government only gave the order for statewide compliance on May 30, 1998 (3). Of course, giving an order to comply when there is no commitment or resources to facilitate compliance is meaningless. A Year 2000 consulting firm, Software Productivity Research, was cited as saying that Russia's Y2K problem would not be resolved for half a century—not until at least the year 2050 (3).

"I'm afraid, there simply is not enough time remaining to alleviate all of the problems," stated Vincent Mullineaux. "*So, I believe our best hope is to alleviate the most critical problems and plan to cope with the rest"* (1). Besides a deadline that is immovable, there are other significant obstacles to successfully eradicating the Bug. There is the fact that old computer code is difficult to read for those programmers unfamiliar with it. Today's programmers do not know where to look for date codes, because so much of it was made-up on site without much standardization nationwide, or even within a company or governmental department. While some "gray-hairs" from the COBOL era are being coaxed out of retirement with nice financial packages, there are too few to make a significant dent in the challenge. There are at least 600 computer languages in use throughout the world with billions of lines of code, each needing to be sifted through "*one at a time"* (4).

Then there are the billions of embedded systems around the world, those tiny microprocessors hidden away in everything imaginable: coffee brewers, microwave ovens, digital watches, answering machines, copiers, faxes, voice-mail systems, smart phones, digital cameras, printers, and scanners. Virtually any hardware using real-time clocks are susceptible to the Bug (5). Also included would be certain machine tools and other plant machinery, measuring instruments and monitors, electronic switches and stabilizers (like those used on oil tankers), and the millions of computerized valves (4, 6). Gartner Group Inc., a Stamford, Conn. Y2K consulting firm, predicts that *"as many as 50 million microprocessors will experience Y2K-related anomalies"* (4).

There is also the obstacle of complacency among many corporate executives and managers—particularly in small to midsize companies—who think they do not have a significant Y2K problem, or that they still have plenty of time to work on it, or that someone somewhere is going to solve the problem. Unfortunately, this complacency also exists in some government agencies and offices, as well as in vital service areas. "*Anybody you speak to who is confident or flippant about this problem . . . those people make me nervous. This is the most unforgiving deadline we've ever faced*," says Peter de Jager (7). Nigel Martin-Jones of Data Dimensions says, "*There are two kinds of people. Those who aren't working on it and aren't worried, and those who are working on it and are terrified*" (2).

Our recent past may even give us a microcosmic view of the future. At the beginning of 1997 some companies experienced production problems costing millions of dollars in damage because some computer programmers forgot to account for 1996 as a leap year (6). Early in 1998, according to *U.S. News & World Report*, 44 percent of U.S. companies had already experienced problems related to Year 2000 failures (4). Computer glitches are not unprecedented, but the Y2K problem is the mother of all glitches, and extends to every nook and cranny of the globe.

Points to Ponder

1. At work and at home, how many pieces of equipment (motorized, machines, appliances, etc.) can you identify that may operate with the aid or control of micro chips?
2. How much have you heard about the Y2K problem from your government (local, state, federal), politicians, business leaders, ministers, etc.? Have you been listening and are you taking them seriously?
3. Have you talked to your family members, neighbors, coworkers, fellow church members about Y2K? If not, why not?
4. Have you seen any Y2K updates or compliance information from your local bank, brokerage, insurance companies, utility provider, law enforcement agencies, emergency and health care providers, or your place of employment?
5. When was the last time you faced a really big challenge in your life, alone or with others, and came out on the other side, better for all the wear and tear?

NEWS FLASH! July 13, 1998. You know about Y2K, the millennium bug. Now meet IF2K.

"Financial firms in Asia are far more concerned with whether they survive until 2000—an issue we have named IF2K—than Y2K systems issues," Tanya Styblo Beder, an analyst at Capital Market Risk Advisors in New York, told a Senate hearing last week. "The problem is that if Asian banks pour all their resources into surviving the current economic crisis, they'll reach the end of 1999 with no Y2K fixes in place and trigger a whole new financial crisis."

Computer World

4

Business (Not) as Usual

But while skeptics say predictions of a day of reckoning are overblown, many business people say so-called Y2K bug is real and menacing(1).

Greg Pessin, Staff Writer
Kansas City Business Journal

The majority of businesses in the United States have gotten off to a late start in addressing the impact of the Year 2000 Bug on their business. Part of the reason is that businesses are driven largely by the bottom line, that is, earnings.

For publicly traded companies, it is those earnings expressed in earnings per share, or EPS, that attracts investors attention. Since the majority of Y2K expenditures subtract from the bottom line and add no short-term value to the company, or for shareholders, many companies have been dragging their corporate feet on thoroughly assessing and correcting their potential Year 2000 problems(2). According to *Business Week*, "*a lot of businesses are in for a nasty shock*" (3).

While the majority of large corporations have been giving the Y2K Bug their utmost attention, and were early on the scene to hire key computer technology people to work on the problem, many midsize, and the overwhelming majority of small businesses have been late to the party, and thousands of them, particularly small companies are not taking the issue seriously enough. The saving grace for some of these smaller companies might be that they have been slow to adapt modern computer technology, and therefore just might have added new computers and software that is Year 2000 compliant. A *Computer World* article states, however, "*The way things are going, your retail shelves will be bare and your assembly line will be missing some key parts come January 2000. Experts say many suppliers are clueless about fixing their systems for the millennium and are headed for failure*" (4). A *Business Week* article in early March, 1998 says: "*a large company or organization that has not yet started dealing with Year 2000 is in big trouble*" (3).

This overall late start in addressing Y2K problems by the business community raises some serious concerns by many Year 2000 experts. The often relied upon Gartner Group, a computer industry research firm in Stamford, Conn., projects that "*half of all businesses are going to fall short*" of their Y2K fix-up needs (4). Matt Hotle, Gartner Group's research director asks: "*What is the impact to the economy of 1 percent going out of business?*" (5). In the same article, Capers Jones, Chairman of Software Productivity Research, Inc. and considered a top Year 2000 expert, was more pessimistic in predicting that 5 percent of all businesses will go bust.

For many businesses, the Y2K battle must be waged on four major fronts:

1. Making sure their computer systems are Year 2000 compliant.

2. Making sure all office equipment (such as fax machines, copiers, printers, phone systems, etc.), machinery, security, and environmental control systems are checked for date-sensitive embedded microprocessors.

3. Getting certification from key vendors and suppliers that they will be Year 2000 ready and will not have interruption in service.

4. Checking and re-checking to make certain that all integrated computer systems, whether in-house, at other business locations, or with other critical businesses and services, such as banking, are ready to run smoothly.

"*The problem with Yr2K*," says David C. Hall, an Embedded Systems Specialist with CARA Corporation in Oak Brook, IL, "*is that the impacts are individual and unique on each enterprise and organization. It is impossible to come up with an average, or a generic, or a template impact analysis. Each enterprise must be assessed on* [an] *individual basis*" (6).

Although a majority of large businesses have made serious headway in fixing their Y2K problems, and have the financial and manpower resources to attack the Bug aggressively, far too many smaller businesses have grossly under-estimated their susceptibility to the Bug and the time and effort it will take to correct the problem. Small, closely held, businesses are particularly vulnerable to a sneak attack by the Bug. Too busy trying to make money, and being the Jack-of-all-trades, many small business owners are either oblivious to the problem, or have not put a priority on eradicating their potential Y2K problems. Quoting a National Federation of Independent Business survey of 500 small businesses, the *Wall Street Journal* reports: "*Despite forecasts by many technical experts of impending chaos, 40% of small businesses say they have no plans to do anything about the possibility of computer glitches on New Year's Day 2000*" (7). The same survey estimated that 82% of the businesses surveyed were candidates for Year 2000 problems in one or more aspects of their business.

Many business owners unfortunately believe they have until December 31, 1999 to deal with the problem. They do not realize that, depending on the size and complexity of their business, the time it takes to assess, fix, test, troubleshoot, re-test, and integrate their computer systems, as well as work on any embedded chip problems, could add up to months and years. To be assured of their readiness, most companies should have their fix-it work completed by fall, 1998, to allow for a comfortable window of testing and working out any bugs. A late start also deprives a company of critical people resources who understand and can effectively fix the Bug problem. Most of those people will be too busy working on some other company's Y2K problems.

Big corporations, while way in front of mid-size and smaller companies in dealing with Y2K, are far from the finish line. A Forrester Research (Cambridge, Mass.) report released in the spring of 1998, stated that *on an average, large corporations were only 34% of the way through their Year 2000 projects*. As a group they had completed only 66% of the task of assessing the breadth of their problem; had completed only 40% of the necessary repairs; and had tested only 18% of their fixes for Y2K effectiveness (8). But fixing a Year 2000 glitch in one place can create problems elsewhere. "*One of the most unsettling aspects of the Y2K bug*," says a *U.S. News & World Report* feature, "*is that fixing the program that runs one piece of equipment can have disruptive effects on other parts of the system*" (9).

Year 2000 problems can be significant and overwhelming for many businesses—just ask General Motors. In the throes of an all-out war against the Bug worldwide, they also had to concentrate on a bitter labor battle in the U.S. that started in the early summer of 1998. In April 1998, GM, the largest manufacturing company in the world, estimated they would spend over half a billion dollars to fix their Year 2000 glitches (8, 10). But William M. Ulrich of Triaxsys Research Group, estimates that GM's cost could be more in the range of $1 billion to $1.5 billion (10). Based on that estimate and the company's Y2K expenditures as of early June, 1998, Ulrich says GM is only 7 percent finished with its Year 2000 Bug problems, and will never make the deadline for completion.

In the same article, GM spokesman, John Ahearne, said the company did not expect Y2K to disrupt production and profitability. Of course, you would not expect him or any other company official to say anything less.

GM's Y2K problems, like that of other large corporations, is not relegated to just their estimated two billion lines of computer code. Like many other manufacturers they must be equally concerned about the thousands, perhaps millions, of embedded microchips in machinery and other factory equipment. When GM sent out ninety-one Year 2000 experts to their 117 plants in 35 countries they were shocked at what the experts found. Says CIO (Chief Information Officer) Ralph Szygenda: "*At each one of our factories there are catastrophic problems . . . machines on the factory floor are far more sensitive to incorrect dates than we ever anticipated* (8).

Dealing with embedded microprocessors poses two enormous problems for manufacturers, according to a *Fortune* article (8). First, although there is some software that can ferret out "00" dates written in COBOL and a few other computer languages, and that can aid in re-coding dates in computer systems, no such aid is available for the billions of embedded systems throughout the world. Second, "*Many embedded programs*," says the *Fortune* article, "*can't be fixed at all because they are inscribed on silicon chips. In some cases, whole pieces of factory equipment, from time clocks to expensive computer-numerically-controlled (CNC) machine tools, have to be junked and replaced.*" Equally daunting, many such chips are in places that are inaccessible to fix-up specialists.

Then there is the problem of a manufacturer's suppliers. Almost all large companies rely on hundreds, and often thousands, of various vendors: from external hardware and software vendors to utilities to banks to transportation, and a host of other service providers (11). GM has 100,000 suppliers worldwide. Will they be ready to meet the giant's daily parts and supply needs without significant interruptions and breakdowns in the supply line? Only time will tell. "*People are playing roulette with their business*," says Peter de Jager (7). In a survey of their customers for Y2K readiness, Honeywell V.P., Rob Baxter said: "*Some plants will have trouble operating and will have to shut down. Some will run at a reduced scope. I expect considerable system outages during December 1999 through February 2000*" (8).

A *Business Week/DRI* economic forecast (based on an estimated Y2K impact) published in the March 2, 1998 issue assumed that 85% of the Year 2000 problems in the nation would be fixed (see chapter 5 on the economic implications of Year 2000). In retrospect, this economic projection may have been overly optimistic. A survey of large companies in December, 1997, indicated that only 2 of 3 businesses had formulated detailed plans for addressing their Y2K problems (3). With small businesses; local, state, and federal governments; and utility companies running far behind, the overall impact on U.S. business, employment, and the economy is hard to predict.

Larry McArthur, President of Ascent Logic Corp., a company that does Year 2000 assessments for companies, said in June 1998, "*Firms only now starting to tackle the Y2K problem should be thinking about triage*" (assigning priorities for urgent attention) (9). A *Mercury News* Washington Bureau article states: ". . . *uncertainties abound. Many private companies are reluctant to reveal the extent of their problems, partly from fear of lawsuits by disgruntled shareholders or customers* (12).

Recent studies by the SEC (Securities and Exchange Commission) of large companies, and by the NASD (National Association of Securities Dealers) of small businesses, were less than encouraging (9). The SEC found that only 42 percent of large companies had even finished an inventory of their critical computer systems that might be susceptible to the Y2K bug. Keep in mind that assessment of the problem is the least problematic for most companies, but still only the first step, after a plan of action, in a potentially long process of rectifying any Year 2000 problems. Among small businesses it is even worse. The NASD found that 61 percent of the companies had not even come up with a Year 2000 plan of action for their business.

Publicly traded companies are also reluctant to reveal their Y2K progress. Triaxsys Research, in an analysis of the top 250 publicly traded companies, states that of the top 250 publicly traded companies only 136 have disclosed any information on their Year 2000 progress. Collectively, their reports reveal that the largest public companies in the U.S. have made remarkably little progress on Year 2000 (12).

Another fly in the ointment is the general lack of preparedness of the business community outside the United States. As a whole, U.S. businesses, despite the late start or no start by the majority in addressing the Y2K problem, are way ahead of the large majority of businesses abroad. In Western Europe, the governments and businesses have largely been preoccupied with their general economies and converting to the Eurodollar. Eastern European nations have been struggling with their fledgling economies, issues of democracy, free trade, and business privatization. Asia and the Far East, including Russia, China, India, Japan, and all of Southeast Asia have been focused on crumbling or troubled economic conditions, as well as democracy challenges. Companies in South America also lag far behind in addressing critical Year 2000 issues and preparedness.

The Herculean effort of American business as a group, notwithstanding, is in various stages of progress and success. There will be many who will satisfactorily complete the process on time, but many more who, still playing catch-up or just getting started, will have to cut corners that may come back to haunt them in the year 2000. Those businesses who have ignored the warnings and chose to do nothing will likely have short tenures in the new millennium.

Points to Ponder

1. Are you aware of your place of employment's Year 2000 plans to become compliant? Is there anything that you can do to help your employer become compliant?

2. Are the people responsible for the Y2K effort at your place of employment making sure that all critical suppliers, services, and vendors will not falter over the Year 2000 problem?
3. Does your place of employment have a Y2K contingency plan for continued operations, both emergency and long-term (3-6 months), if key services are not available, or vendors and suppliers are unable to deliver?
4. If you are laid off from work as a result of Year 2000 problems at work, do you have the financial resources to make ends meet for one, three, six months, or longer? Keep in mind that if your local or state government experiences Y2K problems it may not be easy to collect unemployment or other benefits.
5. What marketable skills do you have in other lines of work if your particular industry is temporarily shut down?

NEWS FLASH! July 8, 1998. *If the threat of your computer crashing isn't enough to spur action, maybe the thought of being sued is.*

The Arizona Republic
"Y2K slackers risk suits, lawyers warn"

5

It's the Economy!

Inevitable difficulties are going to emerge. You could end up with . . . a very large problem (1).

Alan Greenspan, Chairman,
Federal Reserve Testimony,
February 25, 1998
Before the Senate Banking Committee

The U.S. Economy

Many economists, including the venerable Federal Reserve Chairman, Alan Greenspan, appear to be in agreement: the Year 2000 bug will exert a two-prong attack on the U.S. economy, starting as early as the fourth quarter of 1998. What they disagree on is the degree of the economic impact. A small dissenting number believe there will be minimal effect on a currently strong economy. Others see a slight downturn. But a growing number are seeing the possibility of a mild recession to a global-wide recession of significant magnitude.

Prior to January 1, 2000, the attack on the economy from the Millennium Bug will be primarily from the billions of dollars that will be spent by governmental departments and agencies, and the thousands of companies nationwide, to fix their Year 2000 problems. Some impact is likely to be felt from early Y2K failures as fiscal year 2000 arrives for a large number of businesses and government entities during 1999. Because such large sums of capital will have to be diverted, which could be used by governments to provide services, reduce taxes, or cut deficits; and by businesses to increase efficiencies, increase market share, or hire more workers, Chairman Greenspan warns of an economic downturn (2). The Gartner Group estimates that there are 180 billion lines of computer code worldwide that will require screening at a cost of $1 to $1.50 per line. They further project that the top 100 FORTUNE companies will spend an average of $50 million each to correct their Y2K problems (2).

As the economy moves into the year 2000, further disruptions and economic slowdowns are likely to come from continued Y2K spending, potential business failures, or at least some impact on company earnings; and from systems failing due to non-compliant integration with computers abroad. Potentially complicating economic matters could be upwardly spiraling price increases as companies try to recoup their Y2K expenditures; rising interest rates; billions of dollars in law suits from Year 2000 failures; and continued economic turmoil abroad. Larry Burkett, economist and best selling financial author, states: "*I believe the fallout from the year 2000 problem will scuttle all current projections for government revenues and economic activity*" (3).

Vincent Mullineaux, President of Millennia III, in his testimony before the Senate Banking Committee, said: "*In our view this is the single largest business-economic problem this nation has faced since the savings and loan crisis of the 1980s and the energy crisis of the 1970s.*" He further testified that "*the total cost worldwide of dealing with the Year 2000 problem could exceed $1 trillion . . . and global recession if the Year 2000 problem is not minimized*" (4). Ed Yardeni, a sought-after Y2K authority and chief economist for Deutsche Morgan Genfell, Inc., also sees the real possibility of a global recession (5).

There are some dissenters on the view of an economic slowdown in the U.S., notably Lawrence Kudlow, chief economist for American Skandia in Shelton, Conn. Mr. Kudlow believes "*Y2K is flat-earth economics*" (6), that is, "*economic experts have no faith in the wisdom and actions of ordinary people. They think only 'experts' are smart. This view is just as wrong as those medievalists who argued that the earth was flat, and people will fall off the edge into an historical world-ending abyss*" (7).

"*Many experts*," he asserts, "*argue that we know exactly how to solve this problem and thousands of managers are taking steps to do so.*" Mr. Kudlow also believes that the recent GDP (Gross Domestic Product) growth, of which nearly half was comprised of business equipment manufacturing, will help lessen the impact of Y2K on the economy. "*All of the bears* [naysayers] *on this subject, with their flat earth economics*," claims Kudlow, "*are going to be dead wrong again*" (8). For everyone's sake let us hope that Mr. Kudlow is dead right.

Mr. Kudlow, of course, has some formidable opponents to his viewpoint, including Federal Reserve Chairman, Alan Greenspan, who testified before the Senate Banking Committee on February 25, 1998. "*We do not know*," he stated, "*or cannot realistically make an evaluation of what the economic impact is as a consequence of the* [computer] *breakdowns that may occur. We do not know the size. We do not know the contagion and interaction within the system. And we do not know how rapidly we can resolve the problem*" (9). He further said that the Year 2000 problem has already had a negative impact on the economy and warned of a greater impact ahead. Mr. Greenspan was also quick to assure the Committee that the Federal Reserve stands ready to loan tens of billions of dollars to banks who might have trouble making payments as a result of Year 2000 problems.

Chief economist Edward Yardeni also believes that "*The Y2K problem is a very serious threat to the U.S. economy*" (1). Philip Kozloff, of Citibank's Credit Policy Committee is concerned that Y2K failures "*could trigger a whole new round of country debt negotiations*" (10). In a *Newsweek* feature on Year 2000 the concern was expressed that there could be "*severe dislocations because of the mind-boggling enormity of the problem*" (11).

While there is general agreement on the potential for a negative impact of Year 2000 glitches on the U.S. economy, few are willing to quantify the results. Standard & Poor's DRI, in preparing an economic impact analysis for *Business Week*, estimated that Y2K problems would likely reduce the 1999 GDP growth rate by 0.3 percent as more companies diverted their financial resources to fix their Year 2000 problems. In the year 2000 and 2001, they believe the GDP could be cut by 0.5 percent in each year due to the Y2K impact. *"The Year 2000 bug,"* says David A. Wyss, DRI chief economist, *"will certainly hurt the economy, and it could be a real killer if more of the problems are not fixed"* (10).

Our Financial Institutions

Financial institutions—banks, credit unions, loan companies, insurance companies, investment houses, and the like—are the backbone of any economy. Without them, all necessary financial transactions and transfers of payment cease. Recognizing this early in the midst of the Year 2000 hoopla, the large majority of financial institutions and companies got a jump start on addressing potential Y2K problems. As a result, many in the U.S. financial world are confident of a relatively smooth transition to the year 2000. Michael Reddy, head of securities industry Year 2000 unit at EDS Corp. states emphatically: *"There is no chance of the industry not making the changes that are necessary in time"* (12). Others are somewhat more guarded in their viewpoint. Kevin Parker, Head of Information Technology at Morgan Stanley believes that, *"Because of the interconnectedness of worldwide financial institutions, the absolute worst case, albeit highly unlikely, is a global financial meltdown"* (12).

While U.S. financial institutions have been working on the Y2K bug for a number of years, of major concern is the Year 2000 readiness of the global financial marketplace where approximately $3 trillion in currency changes hands electronically every day (13). If these transactions are hampered in any way, or corrupted by faulty systems, the impact on the global financial system could be significant. (See chapter 10 for a brief discussion on how the failure of the Global Positioning System (GPS), a synchronized satellite communication/navigation system, could not only affect private, commercial and military navigation, but the worldwide electronic banking and financial system as well.)

This potential ominous cloud aside, Peter de Jager believes the U.S. financial industry is *"ahead of the game"* in conquering their Year 2000 problems (14). Capers Jones, another Y2K expert and Chairman of Software Productivity Research Inc. notes that, *"The securities and banking industries are the most advanced in terms of year 2000 oversight, monitoring, and coordination"* (15).

Most large financial institutions have the financial resources, and were early enough in dealing with the problem that they were able to secure top Y2K computer programming talent. And they need a lot of both due to the extensiveness and complexity of their computer systems. Take BankBoston as an example. As the nation's fifteenth largest bank it must investigate 60 million lines of computer code for Year 2000 date glitches (11). Smaller banks with less resources, as a group, are lagging far behind in their race against the Y2K clock. Many, who outsource (farm out) a lot of their check processing and other computer-related functions are dangerously assuming that those service providers will be Year 2000 compliant (10).

To the investment industry's credit, seven firms, under the direction of the Securities Industry Association, have already completed a successful Year 2000 trial run. SIA is planning a Wall Street-wide test in July, 1998 (17) and an industry-wide test for March, 1999 (15).

Despite the financial industry's apparent lead over the rest of the nation in confronting and fixing the Y2K bugs, experts are advising the consumer not to be complacent. Many are recommending that you secure a hard copy of all your financial records prior to the last day of December, 1999, just in case your records are inadvertently lost through a computer scramble or shutdown (11). Some financial advisors are also urging prudence by recommending that you have sufficient cash on hand to meet your living needs just in case your local bank or credit union stumbles into the year 2000.

Perhaps of greater concern is the potential impact of a bumpy Year 2000 transition on the U.S. and world financial markets. Although the investment industry in America appears to be well on its way to completing its Year 2000 readiness, a large number of the world's investment firms abroad may not. And, just because the investment industry is ready to roll smoothly with incoming January 1, 2000, it doesn't mean that all the companies whose stock and bonds they trade will be ready for an uneventful transition. Many publicly traded companies have been reluctant or less than informative in reporting to the SEC their readiness for the Year 2000 (16).

Although the U.S. financial industry as a whole appears to be on the Y2K ball, 83% of Year 2000 transition project managers in the United States who were questioned in a March, 1998 Information Technology Association of America survey believe the Dow Jones Industrial Average will fall at least 20 percent once the Y2K crisis unfolds (18). In a survey by CIO magazine, 38 percent of information technology professionals say they plan to pull money out of their banks and investments prior to January 1, 2000 (13). If investors in large numbers follow that lead, a self-fulfilling prophecy of a declining financial market will ensue.

Points to Ponder

1. If you are not afraid of the "R" word, when was the last time you went through a recession? How did it impact your job and your lifestyle?
2. If the majority of the world is not ready to absorb the impact of Year 2000 computer glitches, what effect will it have on your local and state economies?
3. How much of the revenues of the company you work for are generated from outside the U.S.?
4. Are you living in a "company town?" If so, when was the last time a large number of the community were laid off?

5. What plans are you making for your portfolio in the event the financial markets drop more than 10%, more than 20%, more than 30%?

NEWS FLASH! July 14, 1998. *Wall Street took the lead Monday to try to control the Year 2000 computer bug, launching a series of tests to see if U.S. markets will run into disaster in less than 18 months, when 1999 turns into 2000. . . . This is the first known comprehensive effort to check the compliance of corporate America for the so-called Y2K bug. The results could be a road map for other industries and government agencies.*

USA Today Tech Report
"Wall Street passes first Y2K test"

6

Out Go the Lights

I think the chances of regional blackouts and heavy brownout activity throughout the [nation's power] grid are about 80 percent.

Sen. Bob Bennett (R-Utah)
Chairman, Senate Committee,
Year 2000 Technology Problem
June 12, 1998 Hearing

Although today's modern utility plant uses computers for a variety of functions, including billing, and date-sensitive software or embedded microchips in built-in clocks to monitor and control the flow of power, gas, water, and sewage processing, the utility industry has been slow to mobilize Year 2000 task forces. In a June 12, 1998 hearing called by a Senate committee on the Year 2000 Technology Problem, Senate panel members were shocked at the utility industry's lack of preparedness. Of ten large utility companies with a combined customer base of 50 million, only two had even completed an assessment of their Y2K problems. None had developed a contingency plan for utility delivery in the event of a Year 2000 failure (1). While utility companies generally have an emergency mobilization plan for local temporary blackouts caused by storms, a lack of a system-wide power grid contingency plan could spell short-term disaster.

As a result of this surprise testimony by utility industry representatives, Senator Christopher Dodd (D-Conn.) declared, *"We're no longer at the point of asking whether or not there will be any power disruptions, but we are now forced to ask how severe the disruptions are going to be"* (1). Peter de Jager will not rule out power outages as severe as the one that plunged much of the East Coast into darkness in 1965 (2). After hearing this revelation by utility members, Senator Bob Bennett felt that there was a 40 percent chance of a major blackout come January 1, 2000 (1).

In March, 1998, considerably after many other industries were well into addressing their Y2K problems, it was reported that the utility industry was just starting to get a *"handle on the problem"* (3). Despite this late start, and the fact that *"many companies had set compliance deadlines too close to Jan. 1, 2000, leaving too little time to test their modified systems"* (1), utility executives were confident that their plants will be ready to deliver on January 1, 2000 (4). *"We still have 18 months,"* says Sen. Bennett (4). But that is 18 months to develop a plan; assess the problem; find all embedded time-sensitive chips; repair, replace, or scrap affected computer codes and embedded systems; test; troubleshoot; re-test; make adjustments; integrate with other repaired systems; re-test; assure Y2K compliance of all vendors and suppliers; and develop a crack-proof contingency plan. All this, and yet there is no federal regulatory agency that has the authority to force private utility companies to comply with Year 2000 readiness (1).

Electric Power Research Institute representative, Charlie Siebenthal, states, *"We don't know if electricity flow will be affected"* (3). However, as early as spring of 1997, some large utilities were already experiencing Year 2000-related problems. The Hawaiian Electric utility company ran tests during that time to see if they were susceptible to the Y2K bug. Systems analyst, Wendell Ito, said: *"basically, it just stopped working"* (5). In 1998, a Midwestern electric utility ran a Year 2000 test and its safety system mistakenly detected a dangerous operating situation and completely shut down the plant's power generators. Technicians made repeated attempts to fix the problem without immediate success (6). As of early 1998, the executives of Conectiv, a large consolidated East Coast utility, had yet to put Year 2000 compliance on their priority list (7).

"Regulatory agencies are still assessing the year 2000 readiness of utility companies," says James Hoecker, chairman of the Federal Energy Regulatory Commission (1). Shirley Jackson, chairwoman of the Nuclear Regulatory Commission, testified that the NRC does not believe that the Y2K problem will *"have an adverse impact on the ability of a nuclear power plant to safely operate or safely shut down"* (8). A year earlier, however, the NRC conceded that the Bug might affect *"security control, radiation monitoring . . . and accumulated burn-up programs"* [which involve calculations to estimate the hazard posed by radioactive fuel] (5). *"It wouldn't surprise me,"* says Jared Wermiel of the NRC, March 1998, *"if certain plants find that they are not Year 2000-ready and have to shut down"* (3).

Other energy sources, such as natural gas and oil, are also at risk, according to Peter de Jager, and those working in the energy industry (2). In addition to the potential computer problems that most companies face, oil and gas companies rely on thousands of embedded microchips to monitor critical temperature and pressure measurements along their pipelines. Without this ability every few minutes, operators would be flying blind. If any of those sensors failed as a result of Y2K, pipelines would have to shut down to avoid potentially dangerous conditions (2).

A big problem for a lot of energy companies is the location of these sensors. For example, Shell Oil, with miles of pipeline that passes under the North Sea, acknowledges that to reach these frequently placed sensors and replace suspect ones, takes specially equipped divers at a cost of $100,000 per dive (2). A monumental task, whether checking for sensors under the sea, under or above ground, that must be replicated thousands of times by hundreds of energy companies worldwide.

With all the uncertainties, it is no wonder that Mike Hyland, engineering manager at the American Public Power Association asserts, *"No one's going to give you a 100 percent assurance"* that Year 2000 glitches will not affect power. *"Is there a possibility* [of a Year 2000-related power outage]*? At least remotely, yes,"* concedes Hyland (8). Michehl Gent of the North American Electric Reliability Council sees the probability of cascading power outages as *"extremely low, but conceivable"* (8).

A front page article in one small town newspaper boldly proclaimed that the local utility was Year 2000 compliant. This, despite the fact that the utility had not completed its assessment of its potential Y2K problem, nor received any certification that its electric and natural gas suppliers were Y2K compliant, or even working on the problem. For a suggested list of questions you can ask your utility company, as well as other critical community service providers, see chapter 20.

Points to Ponder

1. If there were no electricity coming to your home, what would no longer work in your house?
2. If your furnace stopped working in January how long before your home got uncomfortably cold?
3. If there is no power, then that means there is no water (eventually), which means you would not be able to flush the toilet or take a shower. What would you do?
4. Do you know what the status of the Y2K plan is for your local utility and their power suppliers?
5. Does your utility company have a suitable contingency plan in case their best Year 2000 preparations fail?

NEWS FLASH! July 15, 1998. *In the days leading up to Jan. 1, 2000, Americans should document financial information and stock up on food and essentials, said [Robert Bennett], the U.S. Senator leading the charge for Year 2000 compliance on Wednesday. "Pay attention to the things that are vulnerable in your life and make contingency plans."*

TechWeb
"Bennett Paints Jan. 1, 2000
Scenario"

7

Government Malfeasance

Earlier this month, Rep. Stephen Horn, R-Lakewood [Calif.], chairman of the subcommittee monitoring the problem . . . reviewed all federal agencies' reports on their progress fixing their computer systems. "Overall, the federal government earned an F," Horn concluded.

Mercury News Washington Bureau
"Year 2000 prospects chill Congress"
June 12, 1998

Federal Government Preparedness: Failing the Grade.

Although a number of Year 2000 experts have been sounding the alarm since the mid-1980s (or earlier by some accounts) about an impending computer disaster, politicians at the state and federal level have been slow to respond. Not until February 4, 1998, did President Clinton issue an Executive Order that would create a White House council in an effort to coordinate the government's Year 2000 problem-solving effort (1). This was less than six months from the deadline of June 30, 1998, that many Y2K experts had set as being necessary for Year 2000-susceptible computer systems to be ready to start testing, and a month *after* the deadline recommended by the Subcommittee on Government Management, Information and Technology (GMIT) for Federal agencies to be ready to test their Year 2000-repaired systems. Consultants estimated that it would take a year or more *after* Y2K computer code changes had been made, for entities with larger, older systems to have adequate time to test, troubleshoot, re-test, and integrate the completed changes with other computer systems.

One day later, February 5, 1998, a House panel approved legislation (HR3116) *"to ensure that financial institutions, such as banks and credit unions, are taking the necessary steps to prevent computer chaos"* (1). Apparently it had escaped the attention of the Capitol Hill group that the majority of the financial industry had been working on the problem for a couple of years already. With the speed at which the political community and its bureaucracies move to correct any situation, one can only shutter at the potential outcome.

The Year 2000 preparedness of the U.S. federal government, departments and agencies is of major concern. On April 16, 1996, the Subcommittee on GMIT held a hearing in which subcommittee chairman, Rep. Stephen Horn (R-Calif.) stated that: *"The hearing revealed that there is a serious lack of awareness of the* [Y2K] *problem on the part of a great number of people in business and in government"* (2). As a result, on April 29, 1996, the subcommittee sent a survey to 24 major government departments and agencies to assess their Year 2000 awareness and preparedness. Rep. Horn reported the results of that survey on July 30, 1996 with candor: *"The responses received from Federal agencies, in most cases, provided us with limited information, on when and at what cost agencies plan to correct this potentially disastrous computer software conversion problem. Even with this information,"* Horn continued, . . . [it] *"portrays a Federal government unable to meet the challenges of the 21st century because of a lack of awareness and preparedness."*

The findings of the subcommittee were disturbing at best. Among the subcommittee's findings were that major departments were only in the initial *planning stages* of their Y2K effort, giving them only 18 months to assess and fix millions of lines of code by the recommended testing deadline of early 1998, while the agencies were simultaneously trying to perform agency functions and services. Two of the 24 agencies, **Social Security Administration** and the **Department of Defense**, considered leaders in the government Year 2000 battle, were *"not close to completing the inventory and solution stages of conversion,"* Horn reported. Of the 24, only six agencies, including the **Department of Health and Human Services** and the **Department of Agriculture**, had even assessed the cost of resolving the problems—and for those six, the estimate was $298 million.

As of the survey date, the **Department of Defense** had not yet completed its inventory of the estimated 358 million lines of code that would need to be manually checked for Y2K errors—estimated fix-up cost ranged from $358 million to $3 billion. **NASA**, *"one of the most innovative, advanced and computer dependent agencies,"* Horn said, *"has not prepared a plan to solve the problem and does not anticipate having a plan completed until March, 1997 . . .* [leaving] *less than a year to inventory, and fix systems."*

The **Department of Transportation**, which includes the **Federal Aviation Administration**, **Federal Highway Administration**, and the **Federal Railroad Administration**, Horn reported, *"did not respond to the questions as of this date"* [July 30, 1996]. The Department of Energy *"did not begin to address the year 2000 issue until a week **after** it received the subcommittee's survey,"* Horn commented.

Crisis in Leadership: Too Little, Too Late

So, did the Federal government departments and agencies, and the White House spring into high gear to tackle this national emergency? *"What is the government doing"* [about Y2K preparedness]? *"Not enough,"* declared a *Newsweek* article on June 2, 1997. *"It's ironic,"* said Sen. Fred Thompson (R-Tenn.) in the article, *"that this administration that prides itself on being so high tech is not really facing up to the potential disaster that is down the road a little bit"* (3).

A year later, in a Memo to Congress, Steve Forbes (businessman, 1996 presidential candidate, and Honorary Chairman for Americans for Hope, Growth and Opportunity) wrote, *"the federal government is even more woefully unprepared than the rest of society"* (4). *"The implications are ominous,"* Forbes continues. *"Medicare, the IRS, the Federal Aviation Administration and other basic agencies are operating on utterly out-of-date technology."*

Realizing that 44 of 50 states start their year 2000 fiscal year on July 1, 1999, and the federal government on October 1, 1999, and the unlikelihood that the federal or any state government will be totally prepared for the year 2000, Sherry Burns, director of the Central Intelligence Agency's (CIA's) office Year 2000 effort, commented that: *"As you start getting out into the population, I think most people are again assuming that things are going to operate the way they always have. That is not going to be the case"* (4). Most Y2K experts are convinced that there will be uncertainties and disruptions in local, state, and federal services come January 1, 2000, if not before.

By mid-1998, many federal government agencies had barely completed an inventory of their vast computer systems to determine the size of their Y2K problem—prompting Gene Dodaro of the U.S. General Accounting Office to warn that, *"critical services could be severely disrupted"* (5). In addition, the Office of Management and Budget (OMB), has grossly underestimated the government's Year 2000 fix-up cost, say the experts. OMB estimates a $2.3 billion tab, while Y2K consultants say the cost will run at least $30 billion (3). The technical corrections for Y2K are estimated by the Gartner Group to reach up to $600 billion worldwide. That could go over $1 trillion, they say, with Year 2000 litigation (3).

Once again, in early June, 1998, Rep. Horn reviewed federal agency reports on their Y2K progress, and declared: *"Overall, the federal government earned an F"* (6).

Edward Yardeni, chief economist for Deutsche Morgan Grenfell, stated: *"There is no way we're going to fix 100% of all the computer systems around the world in time . . . My analogy is the 1973-74 recession* [precipitated by an interruption in oil supply] . . . *a disruption in the flow of information, especially if it is critically important information, might similarly disrupt global economic activity and produce a recession"* (4).

With only 63% of the federal government's 7,850 "mission critical" computer systems on target for the Year 2000, Steve Forbes declared, *"this is not a technology crisis; it is a leadership crisis"* (4). With an immovable deadline for resolution of this critical problem, and the federal government, as a whole, so far behind, others might agree with Forbes' sentiment.

"We've still got 18 months," declared Sen. Bob Bennett (R-Utah) in 1998. *"Long enough that things can get a lot worse or a lot better. Right now we're thinking they will get a lot better because of the number of people and resources focused on the problem, but there are no guarantees"* (6). It should be noted, however, that according to experts on the Y2K issue, there is nowhere near the number of people needed working on the Year 2000 problem, nor is there adequate financial resources being spent at any level to fully correct the problem. Y2K experts say that after an assessment of the problem, which can take months, there is the laborious manual task of correcting millions of lines of computer code, line by line. This can take months or years, depending on the size and complexity of the computer systems. Then, there could be up to a year of testing, troubleshooting, and re-testing. Then, of course, there are all those potentially troublesome embedded chips that can be almost anywhere.

Since the majority (44 of 50) of state governments and many businesses operate on a fiscal year of July 1 through June 30, their Year 2000 projects must be fully compliant and ready to go by July 1, 1999. The federal government only has a scant three months more before its fiscal Year 2000 starts October 1, 1999. By June, 1998, only 9 of 24 federal government departments or agencies were on schedule. Some very critical ones—Defense,

Education, Energy, Health & Human Services, Labor, State, and Transportation—it was estimated would not be ready until 2002 or later (5, 7). Health and Human Services had just completed their assessment of their 289 business-critical systems in early June, 1998, and did not expect to have those systems fixed until July, 1999 (7). That would leave them virtually no time for testing and troubleshooting before the government's year 2000 fiscal year arrives October 1, 1999. *Financial transactions* [by the federal government] *could be delayed, airline flights grounded, and national defense affected*, warned the General Accounting Office (6).

As a result of the majority of the federal agencies failing to stay on target or within cost estimates, Edward Yardeni feels the chances of a global recession have risen to 60 percent. *"Some valuable government systems will fail,"* he says (7).

Perhaps the person with the most unenviable position is John Koskinen, the person President Clinton appointed on February 4, 1998, to head the new White House council to coordinate the government's effort to correct the Y2K problem for the various government entities. *"Minimizing the* [Year 2000 problem] *will require a major technological and managerial effort, and it is critical that the United State* [sic] *government do its part in addressing this challenge,"* said President Clinton (1).

As a former OMB deputy director, *"Koskinen's task,"* says a Time magazine article, *"is not just daunting; it's impossible. The feds own roughly one-quarter of all the computers in the U.S."* (8). To make matters worse, *"the studied silence,"* Time says, *"of President Clinton and Vice President Gore on the subject isn't making it any easier to raise the alarm."*

"The silence from the vice president's office," says David Moschella of *Computer World*, *"has been particularly conspicuous. No one in politics has worked harder at developing a technology-centric image. Yet in what is arguably the biggest technology policy issue of the 1997-2000 period, Gore has uttered hardly a word"* (9).

Add to that what Rep. Stephen Horn (R-Calif.) stated: *"Under Koskinen government performance* [for Y2K readiness] *has fallen from a D minus to an F"* (8).

Taxes Away!

Testifying before a House Ways and Means subcommittee on the potential for failure of the IRS (Internal Revenue Service) to fix its Y2K problems, IRS commissioner, Charles Rosotti, stated that such a failure *"could result in catastrophic disruption to taxpayers and the government. Millions of erroneous tax notices, refunds, bills, taxpayer account adjustments, account transactions and financial reporting errors could be generated"* (6). At first glance, one might be tempted to rejoice at the prospects of the IRS having trouble collecting your taxes, until you realize that the federal government operates solely on a pay-as-you-go system for government financing and budgeting. No tax revenue *in*, no government spending or disbursements *out*.

"The Internal Revenue Service is struggling to meet the deadline," reported Business Week (10). Among the potential problems Business Week saw if the IRS is not Year 2000 ready: tax revenue uncollected; returns unprocessed; refunds not sent; compliance, criminal, and audit potential shut down; filing nightmares for taxpayers and small businesses (particularly those with complicated returns).

Many IRS observers do not believe the IRS will be Y2K compliant by January 1, 2000. The department is fighting a tough uphill battle with probably the most "patch quilt," antiquated computer system within the federal government. To make matters even worse, its chief information officer and Year 2000 strategist quit before they could get up a head of steam to address the problem. And do they have a significant problem? According to Business Week, the IRS has to assess 60 million lines of code; has 88,000 separate computer application programs to check, 80 mainframe computers, 1000 midsize, an estimated 130,000 personal computers, and 60,000 pieces of tele-communications equipment (11). To top it off, the department is having difficulty finding and keeping qualified programmers and, in 1998, will have to grapple with hundreds, maybe thousands, of changes to the 1997 Tax Reform Act.

Despite these obstacles, computer specialists say the IRS must be done by the end of 1998 in order for their department to run smoothly come year 2000. By mid-November, 1997, however, the IRS had only completed 10% of the necessary repairs to its computer systems.

Social Security

Due to an inadvertent computer crash back in 1989 when a district office staff member tried to set up a routine repayment plan that went past December 31, 1999, the Social Security Administration has been working on the Y2K problem long before most other government agencies were aware a potential problem existed. The question we should all ask those on Capitol Hill: "If the SSA was tipped off to the Year 2000 Bug's presence almost ten years ago, why is the rest of our government just waking up to the reality of Y2K?"

Yet even with this significant jump on dealing with the problem, the SSA is not expecting to be Y2K compliant until December, 1998 (5).

While it is encouraging that the Social Security Administration feels that it is on target, there is no assurance that their systems will be able to integrate with other critical systems of other government agencies. It is important to remember that the Social Security Trust Fund does not have a single dollar in its account due to the decades of political pilfering to help balance the federal budget. Since 1985 alone, politicians have authorized the "borrowing" of more than $700 billion from the Trust Fund. Not a penny of any of the funds borrowed has ever been repaid. Even with the latest ballyhoo about having a budget "surplus" during the government's fiscal year 1998, the "surplus" was generated by diverting $98.9 billion from the Social Security Trust Fund (12).

At best, Social Security has become the government's put 'n-take ace-in-the-hole to cover up excessive spending. As a put 'n-take financial system, if the *put* (tax revenues) isn't received in a timely manner, the *take* will not be given out in a timely manner. Even a short delay in delivery of the $32 billion per week in government payroll and Social Security checks could cause a major shock to the economy (10). Payments for service-related disabilities made by the Veterans Administration could also be disrupted (5).

It is perhaps a moot point on whether or not the Social Security Administration will be Y2K ready. After all, the checks or electronic transfers to more than 50 million American beneficiaries every month do not come directly from SSA. They are processed and distributed by the Financial Management Service (FMS), a little known agency of the U.S. Treasury Department. The FMS is one of the government's agencies that is the furthest behind on getting Year 2000 compliant. FMS is also responsible for a wide range of financial transactions for almost every government agency. Their Y2K status is of great concern to those in and outside the government.

State and Local Governments

Although the federal government is behind, state and local (county and municipality) governments appear to be even further behind (5, 10). As of early 1998 only about one-third of the states were in decent shape, estimates Larry Olson, CIO for the state of Pennsylvania, which got an early start on their Y2K problem (10). Every vital service and system in the local community must be considered suspect: utility delivery, water delivery and treatment, sanitation systems, law enforcement, security systems at plants and jails, emergency systems, health care systems, communication systems, educational facilities, transportation and highway departments, traffic lights, payroll, public records, etc. All are potentially vulnerable and intertwined with each other at some level. What potentially complicates the Y2K problem at the local level, is the basic lack of understanding by community leaders of the chaos the Year 2000 Bug could cause in their community. Of equal importance, is the lack of financial resources and qualified specialists to help smaller communities deal effectively with the problem. In larger metropolitan areas, while the resources might be there, the process can get bogged down because the task is so overwhelming.

With the majority of states facing a fiscal year 2000 on July 1, 1999, many will hit a brick wall before they can get fully compliant. In Massachusetts, a survey of the state's agencies released February 3, 1998, revealed that over 40% had not even taken the first step toward becoming Y2K compliant (10). In Illinois, by June, 1998, the state as a whole was running behind other large states in its Y2K projects (13). As of March 31, 1998, only 40% of the state's 1,468 agency computer systems were deemed Y2K compliant. Some state governments are so concerned about the potential for Year 2000 failure that they are rapidly passing legislation to limit the state's Y2K liability (13). Many local governments and utilities are quickly increasing their liability insurance. In the ever-increasing likelihood that many state and local governments will not be fully Y2K compliant, the success in helping its citizens weather the Year 2000 storm will depend on the leadership that exists in preparing them for all contingencies.

Points to Ponder

1. If your Social Security, disability income, or veteran's benefit check from the federal government is delayed or doesn't show up in January, 2000, do you have other monetary resources you can rely on?
2. What government services do you count on every day? What would your life be like without them for a day, a week, a month?
3. If you had a big snow storm and your streets did not get plowed, could you get to work, to the grocery store, to grandma's house?

4. If Y2K caused a certain degree of panic and chaos, does your local law enforcement have a riot control plan?
5. The ugly ML words (Martial Law) have come up in some circles of discussion. If that ever happened, what would that mean for you, your family, church, and community?

NEWS FLASH! July 14, 1998. President Bill Clinton gave his *first* public address on the Year 2000 problem today before the National Academy of Sciences. *"Because the difficulty is far-flung as billions of microchips that run everything from farm equipment to VCRs, this is not a challenge that is susceptible to a single government program or an easy fix,"* the President said.

Investor's Business Daily
"Will the Millennium Bug You?"

8

Defend Me Not

We are building an information infrastructure, the most complex the world has ever known, on an insecure foundation.

George Tenet, CIA Director
USA Today
"CIA: Y2K bug poses security risk"
June 25, 1998

Partly due to the Year 2000 Bug, a number of high ranking U.S. military officers and Pentagon officials, consider the nation's defenses to be the most vulnerable they have been in some time. In a memo to Congress on May 15, 1998, Steve Forbes warned that: *"Only 24% of Defense's mission-critical systems have been fixed to date. Only 36% are expected to be fixed by January 1, 2000. At this point, Defense's mission-critical systems won't be completely fixed until 2009"* (1).

By mid-June, 1998, the department had achieved only 29% compliance for its 1,898 critical systems (2). Bill Curtis, who is the Department of Defense's point man on the Y2K offensive, is a 27-year computer programming veteran for the military, who is, in essence, fixing a lot of his own Y2K glitches. While the

Pentagon has been working on its Year 2000 problems since 1995, by the spring of 1998 repairs to only 9% of its vital systems had been completed (3). Curtis admits that most of the military's estimated 2,800 mission-critical systems will not make the Year 2000 deadline.

Equally troublesome, is the manner in which the Pentagon is forced to address this computer problem. Because of the rapidly approaching deadline, the U.S. military, as well as many key businesses, have been forced to set aside normal security precautions in an effort to speed up the Y2K process to become compliant. This greatly worries CIA Director George Tenet and others. In his testimony before the Senate Government Affairs Committee, Tenet warned that this lapse in *"security provides all kinds of opportunities for someone with hostile intent"* to gain information or plant viruses (4). If computer bugs are planted or programs stolen *"it's something you may not know about for many years,"* Tenet said.

Is his concern justified? Unfortunately, yes! Of great concern to the CIA: *"Many of the programmers working on the problem are non-Americans and the programs foreign-produced."* Of particular concern to Tenet: with Y2K problems used as a shield, hackers and foreign enemies can enter U.S. computer systems almost unnoticed because any evidence of their attack might be blamed on Year 2000 glitches. While an internal Pentagon study declared that *"there are no major obstacles which will prevent* [the Trident missiles] *from being totally Year 2000 compliant by Jan. 1999,"* the study did admit that *"a year 2000 problem exists"* with several key military technologies (5).

In an April, 1998 General Accounting Office (GAO) report addressing the Y2K problem, the GAO concluded: *"The impact of* [Year 2000 computer] *failures could be widespread, costly, and potentially disruptive to military operations worldwide"* (1). Already, the military is experiencing Y2K-related failures. *"In an August 1997 operational exercise*, the GAO reports, *the Global Command Control System failed testing when the date was rolled over to the year 2000. GCCS is deployed at 700 sites worldwide and is used to generate a common operating picture of the battlefield for planning, executing, and managing military operations. The U.S., and its allies . . . would be unable to orchestrate a Desert Storm-type engagement in the year 2000 if the problem is not corrected"* (1).

Also of great concern to U.S. defense leaders is the lack of reassurance from Russian leaders that its vast nuclear missile arsenal is Year 2000 fail-safe. Not only has the Russian State Telecommunications committee said that it cannot rectify the Year 2000 problems in the remaining time, but *"U.S. defense officials have issued several warnings of the nightmare scenarios which could ensue if Russian early warning computers malfunction because they have not been programmed to work properly into the next millennium"* (6).

These additional challenges to the U.S. military's effectiveness comes at a time when some observers, both inside and outside the military, feel that our defensive force is at its most vulnerable stage in many years. Not only has military spending dropped drastically in this decade, and dozens of military bases around the world been closed, but the U.S. fighting force is at its lowest numerical level in almost 50 years (7). Retired Army Col. David Hackworth says that the military has been so consumed with peacekeeping, humanitarian, and social reform, that it no longer is an effective fighting force. Morale is reported to be low and re-enlistments by career military personnel are way down. Commanders say that replacement parts for fighter jets and other key military equipment are hard to find and they are often forced to strip several pieces of equipment to get one that functions properly.

According to some, the long accepted standards of basic training have been lowered. *"We are beginning to see anecdotal evidence of readiness issues in some units, particularly at the tactical level of operations,"* says Gen. Hugh Shelton, chairman of the Joint Chiefs of Staff. *"The Clinton administration,"* says Thomas Moore, director of the Heritage Foundation's new Military Integrity Project, *"has starved the military materially and undermined it morally."* By these measures, and the challenge of

Y2K, it may take a while to rebuild the pride and capability of our military defenses.

The question that some on Capitol Hill, as well as Y2K experts, are asking, could a Year 2000 disruption bring about martial law in our nation? The quick answer is: Yes! Absolutely! And it appears the Clinton administration is making plans for just such a possibility. But, if needed, will the military, with all its Y2K problems and dwindling moral, be ready, willing, and up to the task?

It appears clear that President Clinton and his administration have been preparing for such an eventuality for some time. In addition to Executive Orders in place since the Kennedy administration, President Clinton has signed more Executive Orders than any other U.S. president—orders that give the President or the military, and various federal government agencies, control of every facet of daily life and commerce in the event of a national emergency. One of the most recent was Executive Order 13083 on federalism, which according to an *Investor's Business Daily* editorial on July 24, 1998, ran roughshod over U.S. Constitution Amendments IX and X, which gives certain rights and responsibilities to individual states and their residents.

If you want more details, visit Gary North's Web site at: http://www.garynorth.com/y2k/results_.cfm/martial_law or read Joseph Farah's "Between the Lines" column at World Net Daily: http://www.worldnetdaily.com. Mr. North's site provides links to detailed information on Executive Orders, while Mr. Farah's column keeps the public informed on new Executive Orders and Directives from the White House.

Of particular importance and concern is the recent Presidential Decision Directive #63 on "Critical Infrastructure Protection" signed by President Clinton and released as a White Paper by the White House on May 22, 1998 (see Addendum 7 for a complete White Paper reprint of the Directive). The Directive was drafted as a plan to provide *essential national security missions* in the event of a threat or collapse of *cyber-based information systems* in the year 2000 or beyond. The Directive further establishes the

National Infrastructure Protection Center, which includes the FBI, the Secret Service and other federal law enforcement agencies, the intelligence agencies, and the Department of Defense.

So, if the White House and various government agencies, and politicians are seeing Y2K as a serious enough threat to prepare for the possibility of martial law, then you can bet it is a serious threat, and one not to be taken lightly.

Points to Ponder

1.Do you know someone in the U.S. military for a career? What have they said about military moral and combat readiness?
2. Has the U.S. government gone too far in liberalizing trade and technology-sharing policies when it comes to our national security?
3. Is it in our best interest to share Y2K technology with former or current avowed enemies of the U.S. in the hope that they will use it for the right purposes?
4. At a time when U.S. military leaders are saying our defenses are vulnerable, should we be selling military and satellite technology to outspoken foes of democracy?
5. Is your local civil defense unit active and prepared for a civil emergency?

NEWS FLASH! July 15, 1998. *To keep any still possible nuclear war, or even some lesser military confrontation, from happening due to the Millennium Bug, the United States and Russia are cooperating to prevent any miscalculations occurring from false computer information. . . . Pentagon spokesperson Kenneth Bacon said . . ."We have offered to share or engage in joint early warning projects with Russia, and maybe with other countries as well."*

CNNfn NEWSBYTES
"US Govt. To Swap Y2K
Info With Russian
Military"

9

TRIAGE OR FLAT LINE?

Experts are predicting more trouble in the health sector, as patient billing and insurance records at hospitals or HMOs are vulnerable . . . patient-monitoring devices are also in danger of malfunction.

U.S. News & World Report
"Year 2000 time bomb"
June 8, 1998

When it comes to health and health care of the nation, the Year 2000 Bug raises its ugly head in three broad areas: payment disbursement to the care facility, the operations of the health care facility, and sanitation issues facing each community. Without payment for services, distributions from sources such as Medicare, Medicaid, insurance companies, and most health care providers would be in dire financial straits within a short period of time. The ability to provide health care and get paid for it will depend on each facility's Year 2000 compliance for billing, patient care and records, medical devices, building equipment (including environmental systems, elevators, office equipment, etc.), and the reliability of vendors and other outside services (including, but not limited to, telecommunications, ambulance and other emergency services, utilities, sanitation, etc.). Lack of sanitation would also be a major threat to any health care provider, whether it be sewage services or waste disposal.

The health care network in the United States, an almost $2 trillion industry, includes hospitals, clinics, doctor's offices, long-term care and assisted living facilities, managed care organizations, payers, third party administrators, laboratories, pharmacies, medical device and equipment manufacturers, etc. (1). A breakdown in the chain of supply or service in any one of these health care-related areas could have disruptive to severe consequences.

While the health care industry as a whole was initially slow to react to the pending Year 2000 crisis, most are moving ahead rapidly to address their problems, often forming coalitions with other providers, vendors, and outside services to battle the bug. One such non-profit organization, Rx2000 Solutions Institute in Minneapolis, MN, established in November, 1996, is dedicated to the health care community to provide supplier compliance information, training and education, vendor matching, and supplier matching (see Addendum 6 for more information).

Another coalition of public and private health care providers made up of the U.S. Department of Veterans Affairs, the American Medical Association, the American Hospital Association, and the American Nurses Association, have urged manufacturers of medical devices to notify their customers of their devices Y2K compliance, or lack thereof, no later than January, 1999 (2). This prodding was needed because medical groups were complaining that the notification process from their medical device vendors was too slow and would put their patients at risk. Medical device makers "*need to take immediate action*," said Kenneth W. Kizer, VA undersecretary for health. "*It's going to take time to address some of these problems. This isn't information that can be made available on December 31, 1999,*" he added (2).

One medical rumor that needs to be squelched: that thousands of pacemakers are in jeopardy of stopping come 12:01 AM on January 1, 2000. Medical experts say users of such devices do not need to worry. Pacemakers are designed to function according to cardiac cycles and not calendar dates (3). It is more likely, experts say, that the read-out devices for pacemakers may produce faulty data if not Y2K compliant. If you have concerns, consult your doctor. Although these devices are safe, many other medical devices in health care facilities across the country will need close scrutiny.

"It's not just their information systems or their billing systems or those that people normally think about with PCs," says Sheila Robida, year 2000 project manager for the Connecticut Hospital Association. *"This kind of* [computer] *logic is also in microprocessors that are embedded in different types of equipment that hospitals and health care organizations use. The problem becomes identifying where all those microchips lie in things like infusion pumps and lab equipment, magnetic resonance imaging equipment, those types of things* (4).

According to Anthony Montagnolo, vice president for technology planning for ECRI, a non-profit private agency that evaluates medical devices for Y2K compliance for health care providers, *"most medical devices will work just fine. But they may have documentation problems by stamping the wrong date on the patient's medical records"* (3). With legal liability for device failure hovering just over the heads of doctors and care providers, ECRI is strongly urging all hospitals to check every piece of equipment on their premises for Y2K bugs.

Although they have picked up the pace, *"Health care in general is probably behind the curve,"* stated Craig Jones, Executive VP of the Oklahoma Hospital Association. *"But there are so many unknowns. Many people are talking in 'what ifs,'"* Jones said (5). With many hospitals just starting to address the problem, and with so few trained programmers left to tackle the problem, some hospitals are likely to fall short of their compliance mark (3). Dr. Ian Cummings, head of the Association of Emergency Physicians, feels that most computer problems will involve patient billing and scheduling, rather than direct clinical care issues (3).

However, manufacturers and vendors of medical devices are slow to respond to inquiries as to the Y2K readiness of their equipment or devices. After four letters requesting Year 2000 information from 1600 manufacturers used by the Veterans Administration, Kenneth Kizer says that they are still waiting for a reply from 30% of them. The FDA (Food and Drug Administration) in querying 16,000 device makers worldwide, had only heard from 11% of them by July, 1998 (2). While many do not supply the VA with Y2K-sensitive devices, such as tongue depressors or latex gloves, they still could have their manufacturing or deliveries disrupted due to Y2K irregularities on their end.

Having absolute certainty of the Year 2000 readiness of critical medical devices is vital to the health care providers. *"I'm surprised,"* says Dr. Alan Spacone, emergency medicine information service consultant for MacNeal Health Network in Berwyn, Ill., *"at how many defibrillators aren't Y2K compliant and how many manufacturers no longer support them"* (3).

William Woloszyn, an information systems specialist with the Integris Health System in Oklahoma, estimates that 40% of their medical equipment is affected by Y2K embedded chips (5).

According to the Oklahoma Hospital Association, 5-10% of patient care equipment, 20-25% of building systems, and 40-50% of computer software are not compliant. *"While quite a few* [vendors] *are forthcoming,"* says Woloszyn, *"some have left no forwarding address and have disappeared."*

One of the biggest problems for health care facilities is knowing how to deal with vital services that are somewhat beyond their control. Today's health care providers are so intertwined electronically with other services, such as pharmacies, ambulance service, insurance carriers, utility providers, food services, etc., that a breakdown in any area for more than a short period could cause significant problems. For example, MacNeal's information network is totally dependent on its telecommunications provider, Ameritech Corporation, but Tom Brogan, MacNeal's director of network systems, says he has been unable to get Year 2000 compliance documentation from the vendor (3).

Another complication for health care providers is a new federal mandate, The Health Insurance Portability and Accountability Act of 1996, that requires them to adopt new standards for electronic transactions by the year 2000 (6). While the end goal of the legislation is to lower health care costs, many health care groups, bogged down with Y2K projects, are largely ignoring the mandate, opting to pay stiff fines and carry out their mandate implementations after assurance their Year 2000 projects have achieved success.

Like many other businesses and organizations, the health care industry must be concerned about the Y2K bug on many fronts. Despite the late start, they know that compliance is critical to the overall health and viability of their respective communities, and are working feverishly to eradicate the bug.

Points to Ponder

1. How prepared are you to handle medical emergencies at home? How prepared is your place of employment to handle medical emergencies?
2. What are the contingency plans for emergency health care in your community?
3. If there is no telephone service how would you contact emergency services?
4. If sanitation services (primarily sewage and waste removal) breakdown, what are your alternatives?
5. Do you have on-going medical needs that you need to plan ahead for in case certain health services or medications are not readily available?

NEWS FLASH! July 16, 1998. *"I won't say we've got it all together and under control,"* said Sheila Robida, Y2K project manager for the Connecticut Hospital Association. *"But if each health institution pays close attention and gets their information* *together, there will be minimal problems. . . ."*

"But no matter how much attention we pay [to testing software]," said Diane Caesar, chief information officer for computers at Englewood [New Jersey] Hospital and Medical Center, *"there will be something that will fail, and contingency plans are being developed for those potential failures."*

The Bergen [NJ] *Record*
"The newest bug hospitals must fight is electronic"

10

Hello? Anybody Out There?

What we do know is that every company, every government agency, and every organization that has looked into the [Y2K] *problem has found that it is more complicated, more serious, and more costly than originally estimated* (1).

William E. Kennard,
Chairman Federal Communications Commission

Have you ever gotten irritated when you just had to get through to someone on the phone and keep getting a busy signal? When January 1, 2000 arrives we better all hope that there is a dial tone or a busy signal, and not just dead silence. Telephone companies across the continent are trying to assure their customers and the FCC (Federal Communications Commission) that everything will be okay, but no absolute guarantees can be offered. After all, none of us, including the telecommunications industry has ever come to such a formidable bridge before. Today, phone company lines are far removed from the old two, three, and multi-party telephone lines that your parents and grandparents grew up with during Ma Bell's days of puberty. Now, telecommunication lines and satellite transmissions carry not only traditional phone calls, but wireless communication, television, intra-office conferences, millions of E-mail and Web site explorations daily. They transmit everything from financial information to financial market trades worldwide. They electronically transfer millions of paycheck deposits and automatic drafts for insurance and mortgage payments, and pre-authorized bank drafts into millions of investment accounts every day.

How important are these various transmissions today? Just ask the 50 million owners of pagers that abruptly stopped working one day in the spring of 1998 when the PanAmSat satellite transmitting their messages went on the blink. Without vital telecommunication hook-ups, life and commerce as we now know it would come to a screeching halt. Imagine what your day would be like without a phone. You couldn't call home to check on the baby-sitter; call into work "sick"; make that big international sale for your company; call your stock broker to tell him or her to "sell, sell, sell!" or "buy, buy, buy!" You would not be able to dial "911" or for any other type of emergency assistance; call Mom and Dad and wish them a "Happy 50th." But most importantly, you wouldn't be able to call out for pizza delivery on Friday night, or any other night. Then what would you do?

If your place of employment does not have phone service or other telecommunication services, how long before you are unemployed? *"If we have major network outages due to Year 2000, many small- and medium-size businesses could find themselves in dire economic straits,"* says FCC Chairman, William E. Kennard (1). So far, despite spending hundreds of millions of dollars on addressing their Y2K problems, telecommunications companies are being rather tightlipped about their Year 2000 progress, or the potential impact on the nation's communication systems if they fall short of reaching Y2K compliance. The problem for the telecom industry is immense. AT&T alone, is expecting to spend $500 million or more on fixing its Y2K problems (2). Deregulating the telephone industry years ago may have been great for consumers, but it has potentially created a Year 2000 nightmare as hundreds of telecommunications and cable TV providers across the nation (and the world) grapple with the complexity of their inter-connectedness.

"Federal officials are making it known," says Anne Howe, writer for Solution Works, *"that the Year 2000 bug could cripple the*

foundation of the telecommunications industry globally and plunge the world into economic, political and technological chaos" (1). She further writes that, *"Industry experts predict more than half of the major U.S. carriers will experience at least one failure of a mission critical system because of a Y2K problem . . . the possibilities of error are enormous."* Not only are all carriers' computer operated systems in jeopardy, but much of the telecommunications equipment at home, in government offices, at medical centers, businesses, trade centers, and everywhere else could be at risk. Some carriers are trying to reassure customers that everything will work out just fine, but none have carried out extensive Y2K testing as of mid-1998.

The FCC, and many others close to the Year 2000 problem, have serious concerns about how the Y2K bug might affect our national preparedness, military readiness, public safety, emergency and personal communications. The U.S. Emergency Alert System, which relies on television and radio broadcasts, *"may fail when it is needed most,"* Kennard says (1). Also of concern to the FCC is the network of nearly 30 synchronized satellites orbiting the earth as part of the Global Positioning System (GPS). Primarily used for navigation and positioning in military maneuvers, GPS also guides shipping and GPS-equipped vehicles. While the concerns about the GPS are not exactly Y2K-related, they are similar due to the internal calendars used in GPS satellites. The FCC is working closely with GPS satellite companies to ensure that transmissions remain uninterrupted on January 1, 2000 and thereafter.

Of grievous concern to the FCC, the Department of Defense, and others that depend on the GPS, is the reality that the system's clocks will roll back and reset to zero by August 22, 1999. At that point, the receivers of GPS signals will read the year as 1980. While a replacement system is under development by Boeing, it will not be ready until the end of 1999 at the earliest. With the worldwide banking industry also relying on GPS for the electronic transfer of trillions of dollars around the world daily, the prospects for financial collapse are ominous.

Although the FCC and telecommunications companies are doing everything possible to attain Y2K compliance, the integrated task of reaching that goal is so enormous that *"it seems improbable that communications companies will have the time to fix all the Y2K related issues,"* writes Howe (1). The potential for a communications breakdown, particularly in developing countries, has caused FCC Chairman Kennard to warn: *"this could have a huge impact on international trade, foreign investment, the global economy and even national security . . . these countries are only now becoming aware of the Year 2000 problem and they lack the resources to fully address it"* (1).

Points to Ponder

1. How many times a day do you use the telephone at home? At work? How many of those calls do you feel are absolutely necessary for your comfort and survival?
2. Have you ever been without phone service for more than a day? What did you do?
3. If you had to go a week, a month, or longer without a phone at home, what would be your alternative for communication with the "outside" world?
4. If, at the same time, there was no electricity, therefore ruling out other forms of communication, such as E-mail, what could you use in case of emergency?
5. How severely would the lack of phone service affect your place of employment, and how expendable is your position?

NEWS FLASH! June 16, 1998. *Time dimensional testing* [for telecommunication companies] *is critical to the success of a Year 2000 project. However, it is very difficult to accurately simulate Year 2000 conditions, therefore companies have fallen behind in their testing. Beware of simplistic solutions that will not properly simulate a post year 2000 environment, or, even worse, a simplistic tool that spawns new programming and development projects to make it work.*

Joe Allegra, President
Princeton Softech
Year 2000 Testing Symposium
(for telecommunication companies)

11

HONK! HONK! BUT NOWHERE TO GO

We're still in the assessment stage . . . Federal Aviation Administration.

Newsweek
"The Day the World Shuts Down"
June 2, 1997

You're up bright and early with renewed enthusiasm for a prosperous new year. You grab a quick few bites of your morning toast and jam, gulp down some orange juice, snatch your travel mug of coffee, and head for the car to start your daily trip to work.

After buckling in first (you're very conscientious that way), you turn the ignition key, but no go. You try and try again, but nothing. Nervous about being late, you decide to try and catch a lift into town from your neighbor. The phone is still dead so you go next door to find him leaning over the engine compartment of his car grumbling loudly. His car won't start either. After trying his car and yours several more times, you both decide to call for a taxi, but his phone doesn't work either. Then you remember that while you have never had to take the local bus, there is one that stops a few blocks away. You and your neighbor, now joined by a few other frustrated area residents, start hoofing it to the bus stop to catch the 7:25. Twelve minutes later you all arrive at the bus stop, a little warm and out of breath, but none the worse for wear.

The crowd at the bus stop seems large to you, larger than the bus seating capacity. The constant conversation of the crowd is filled with tension and frustration. It is now 7:40 and no bus has arrived. You and many others there now realize that your choices for transportation to work have been quickly narrowed down to the old soft shoe. In January, or any other month, the thought of walking 20 miles to your workplace is not a pleasant consideration. What now?

Transportation—personal vehicles, farm equipment, airlines, trucking, buses, trains, ships, recreational and sporting vehicles, etc.—are vital to our way of everyday life. Without one or more modes of transportation, as with telecommunications, our nation's commerce and way of life would come to a standstill. As equally important, in the United States' transformation into an information service economy, we have become so dependent on foreign trade—both export and import—that any significant disruption in trade would have a major impact on our economy and reliance on the conveniences of life to which we have become so accustomed.

In the good old USA, separating us from our automobile is akin to horse thievery. The auto is part and parcel of the American way of life. But today's modern automobile, and all its personal transportation cousins, are computerized wonders that are a far cry from the Model T of yesterday. According to some, today's car could have as many as one hundred microprocessor chips embedded everywhere. *"If they are calendar-challenged,"* experts say, *"forget about driving"* (1).

Your personal transportation aside, public and commercial transportation do not exist in a vacuum by themselves. They depend on many integrated services, vendors, and electronic gadgetry for dispatch, delivery, emergency service, inventory control, etc. The Union Pacific Corp. (railroad) in Omaha, it has been reported has 16,000 outside vendors that it has been checking on for Y2K compliance. They have cut their list down to 800 critical suppliers, but as of March, 1998, only 60 percent had responded to the railroad's Year 2000 inquiries. *"The least responsive, at 17%, were service vendors, such as utilities and banks"* (2). But what worries some railroad veterans the most are the computerized trackside event recorders, and the black boxes on locomotives. Another concern expressed by railroad officials and others, are the railroad crossing gates that are controlled by microprocessors. If they malfunction due to Y2K problems they could freeze in the *up* position even when a train is coming—assuming, of course, that trains will be running.

Despite the FAA's Y2K chief, Ray Long's assurance that *"there's no doubt in my mind that we're going to meet our* [Year 2000] *deadlines"* (3), a poll of technology executives by *CIO* magazine, said that over half would avoid flying on January 1, 2000 (4). One possibility, says *Newsweek*, is that the FAA's computers could lock up if not Y2K compliant. Although planes will keep flying, the systems monitoring them could lock with planes disappearing from view on the screens of air traffic controllers (1). Although one would not expect anything other than optimism from Long, the fact is that the FAA only completed its Year 2000 compliance inventory in March, 1998. At that pace, government auditors said the FAA will not make the compliance deadline for solving all its Y2K problems (4).

The FAA is not alone in struggling to reach compliance. In an early 1998 survey of 44 major airlines serving the U.S., the International Air Transportation Association found that *"only 67 percent expected their systems to be fully Y2K compliant by Oct. 1, 1999."* To which IATA Director General, Pierre Jeanniot, warned: *"Failure to act decisively could have catastrophic consequences"* (4).

Any delays in compliance could compromise airline safety, delay flights, and increase customer inconvenience and cost. *"The FAA will make it,"* says John Koskinen, chairman of the President's Council on Year 2000 Conversion, but he adds, *"we can't dismiss the gloom-and-doomers"* (5).

Points to Ponder

1. What is your main mode of transportation? Currently, how reliable is it to meet your daily needs?
2. If you had to go without it, could you still get to work, to the grocery store, to your doctor's office, to the hospital emergency room?
3. If, come January 1, 2000, your car runs just fine, but gas stations are unable to pump gas, then what?
4. Or, if you have a mechanical or computer chip problem with your car but your mechanic can't fix it because his computerized diagnostic equipment is on the blink, who would you call?
5. How long can you go without your customary mode of transportation and still bring home a paycheck and meet your family's needs?

NEWS FLASH! June 15, 1998. *The FAA has plans to ground planes if its air-traffic system isn't repaired— and it may have to carry them out. The government's own accountants complained earlier this year that "at its present rate, the FAA will not make it."*

TIMEcom
"Why The Government's Machines Won't Make It."

12

The World's Cure

There is a way that seems right to a man, but in the end it leads to death.

Proverbs 14:12

It has been said of modern day people, that whatever we can imagine we can achieve. Over-burdened with our technology and constant clamor for worldly things, we have convinced ourselves that given enough time, money, and manpower, we can accomplish anything our minds can dream up, or our hearts desire. There is no doubt that the technological age has propelled us forward at lightning speed into areas we couldn't fathom or understand thirty short years ago. Such advances have brought us conveniences and prosperity that our parents and grandparents never had, or in many cases, never desired. But technology creates want, rather than need, and most of our new-found wealth is consumption-driven—

much with reckless abandon of common sense and biblical principles. There seems to be no limit to humanity's abilities, intelligence, and absolute cleverness—until now.

Does the Y2K scenario sound strangely familiar to you—maybe from something in the Book of Genesis?

> *Now the whole world had one language and a common speech.*
> *Then they said, "Come, let us build ourselves a city, with a tower that reaches to the heavens, so that we may make a name for ourselves and not be scattered over the face of the whole earth."*
> *The LORD said, "If as one people speaking the same language they have begun to do this, then nothing they plan to do will be impossible for them.*
> *Come, let us go down and confuse their language so they will not understand each other."*
> *That is why it was called Babel—because there the LORD confused the language of the whole world.*
>
> (Genesis 11:1, 4, 6, 7, 9a)

Could the Year 2000 computer glitch be our modern day version of the Tower of Babel? The parallels are striking. Through the great advances in computer and telecommunication technology, we have united the peoples of the earth instantaneously through the wizardry of computers—one language of scientific expression. Technology, wealth, power, and control of our destiny has been and is our pursuit, our avocation. Through most of it we have left God out of the picture as we strive for self-fulfillment.

> *The Lord says: "These people come near to me with their mouth and honor me with their*

> *lips, but their hearts are far from me. Their worship of me is made up only of rules taught by men.*
> *Therefore once more I will astound these people with wonder upon wonder; the wisdom of the wise will perish, the intelligence of the intelligent will vanish."*
>
> (Isaiah 29:13-14)

Now, once again, the (computer) language of the world will be *confused*. Our cleverness has, once again, out-foxed us.

This is not the first modern day crisis that the world has faced, but it is by far the largest, and potentially most devastating. Faced with this challenge, what has been the world's response? Have they turned to God for wisdom and guidance? Have they repented of their evil ways and for rejecting God? Not in the least. Many have chosen to ignore the Y2K problem, thinking that it does not concern them, or that, somehow government or some computer whiz is going to take care of it, or if they just do not think about it, the problem will go away. Others who are more intimately acquainted with the seriousness of the Year 2000 problem have colleagues in business and government who seem convinced that with enough time, manpower, and money, the problem can be solved. However, few are calling the nation and the world to seek God and His wisdom and mercy.

To understand man's approach to this massive problem we must segregate its components: time, manpower, and money. But first, let us take a look at the enormity of the task.

The TASK

It has taken 40-plus years to create the "Information Age" of computer technology and the closely allied telecommunications industry. This technology, particularly in the past ten years, has expanded at warp speed around the globe. With it, the Year 2000

Bug has been reproduced millions of times into millions of computer systems. Many of the computer programmers around the world who originally developed much of today's computer science and inadvertently programmed in the Y2K date glitch, are either retired or dead. With over an estimated 600 computer languages in existence today (1), the size of the task exceeds comprehension for even the experts. To further complicate the task, much of the computer coding used for calendar dates in older languages were custom designed on-site, and was only limited by the programmer's imagination and inventiveness.

The immense task, however, does not stop with a Y2K problem with computers. It extends to the billions of embedded microchips worldwide in every conceivable electronic or computer-controlled device. The list is almost limitless. It is a task so huge that no one, not even the experts on Y2K are willing to venture forth with an accurate scenario for the outcome.

The one thing that the experts seem to agree on about these microchips: no one knows for sure how many of them are out there affecting our life, or how many will have Y2K problems come January 1, 2000, or sooner. The broad estimate, is that there are 10-40 billion embedded chips in use around the world—with as many as 400 million estimated to have Y2K problems; and in such readily inaccessible places as satellites above the earth, and miles of pipeline below the seas. *"If you're trying to test which of these have an actual problem,"* said Bruce Webster of the Washington DC Y2K Group that advises government and business on the Year 2000 problem, *"you're looking at having to examine and test 20 million* [microchips] *per day over the next 18 months"* [based on 25 billion chips] (2). That task of checking out all microchips, alone, is virtually an impossible task to complete on time.

If you are expecting the government to solve this problem, they will not—at least not in any manner that you would appreciate. Will Bill Gates of Microsoft, or some other computer whiz kid, come riding in on a white horse with a "silver bullet" that will clean up everything? *"The reality of this problem,"* says Peter de Jager, *". . . the size of this task . . . means that this is not something that can ever be solved by one single* [computer] *program. There are 500* [some say 600] *computer languages in the world. . . . It* [the Y2K problem] *is not susceptible to a single miracle"* (2).

The TIME

Two things are known and conceded by all Y2K experts about the amount of time needed to correct this gargantuan problem—there is not enough of it, and the deadline for being ready is immovable. This is not like some deadline at work where, if unforeseen circumstances arise, the deadline for completion of a project might be pushed back, or the project modified or reduced to meet the deadline. Neither of those approaches will work with the Y2K deadline. The target date for completion cannot be altered one second, much less a day, a week, or a month. The nature of the project cannot be simplified, modified, or changed, or the negative outcome will be magnified even more.

"I'm afraid there simply is not enough time remaining to alleviate all of the problems," said Vincent Mullineaux, Founder and President of Millennia III, in his testimony before the Senate Banking Committee on February 19, 1998 (3). There is not enough time to *discover* all of the Year 2000-related problems, much less fix and test them. Capers Jones, another highly respected Y2K expert and head of Software Productivity Research, has estimated that to find, fix, and test all the software potentially affected by the Year 2000 bug would take the skilled technical labor of 700,000 person-*years* (4). Simply put: THERE IS NOT ENOUGH TIME!

The MANPOWER

In the past couple of years, businesses and governments have hired hundreds of thousands of information technology and computer specialists to deal with the Year 2000 problem and its related issues. Yet an early 1998 study released by the Information Technology Association of America declared that there were 350,000 job vacancies in the U.S. alone for computer scientists and programmers that were not getting filled (4). This leaves many smaller businesses, some government entities, and latecomers to the Y2K festival of programming needs out in the cold. As a result, many such groups are relying on less skilled personnel in-house, or have even tabled their Year 2000 fix-up projects, hoping to muddle through somehow.

Many large corporations, the federal and some state governments, desperate for Y2K programming help, have forgone their normal security procedures and have, as a group, hired hundreds of thousands of foreigners from countries like India and Pakistan—countries hungry for business and military technology. Some companies and organizations who realize the worldwide shortage of skilled programmers, are trying, as a last ditch effort, to re-train anyone with some computer skills, as computer bug decoders. Despite their best efforts, with a shortage of time and knowledgeable labor to de-bug the bug, there will be too many companies, organizations, and government agencies and departments that will not make the Y2K deadline.

The MONEY

Although some in the United States would have us believe that money is not an obstacle to solving this problem, for many businesses and governments, both in and outside the U.S., the lack of financial resources, or in the case of business, the impact to their profitability, is a definite roadblock to their Y2K readiness.

The Gartner Group was one of the first to try and put a financial face on the Year 2000 Bug. Their estimates on the worldwide financial impact of the Y2K problem have been frequently quoted as between $300 to $600 billion, and potentially over $1 trillion, if you add in the purchase of new hardware and software, and the inevitable cost of litigation over Year 2000 losses as a result of an entity's non-Y2K compliance (5). While there have been lower estimates by the General Accounting Office and others, Gartner's numbers are generally accepted by most, and a few even argue that they may be conservative.

For many businesses with narrow cash flows, trying to squeeze out money for a Y2K project that they are not yet convinced will impact their business, will likely prove to be a disastrous decision. With many national economies abroad struggling for survival until the year 2000, they find it hard to justify spending millions or billions they really do not have on a problem that seems to them to be eons away.

Two questions that beg asking in the light of all this. 1. Could this forestall or hasten the One World Order (Government)? 2. Could it forestall or hasten a world cashless society? If it is a crisis of God's design—through man's own foolishness—to be used for His purposes, then we can all pray that this will forestall or scrap these errant notions of man. If, on the other hand, this is a crisis purposely designed by man to enhance his god-like objectives, then this crisis might only hasten those objectives.

13

But Seek First ...

For the wisdom of this world is foolishness in God's sight. As it is written: "He catches the wise in their craftiness."

(1 Corinthians 3:19)

From a biblical or Christian perspective we could spend a lot of time discussing the Y2K problem and the reason we have it. Is it the foolish oversight of a few technology wizards in the beginning—and many since then? Is it man's sinfulness and rebellion against God? Is it a calculated plan of some diabolical group? Is it a fulfillment of prophecy? Whatever the reason or reasons, the reality of the Y2K problem is that it is here, and we are all confronted with dealing with it. The good news, if you have accepted Jesus Christ as Lord and Savior, is that Jesus says: *"I have told you these things, so that in me you may have peace. In this world you will have trouble. But take heart* [be of good cheer, KJV]*! I have overcome the world"* (John 16:33).

God will not violate our will in this matter of Y2K, or any other matter. He desires to meet our needs, but we must seek him and ask him. Once again, Jesus, in Matthew 6:31-34, says:

> *"So do not worry, saying, 'What shall we eat?' or 'What shall we drink?' or 'What shall we wear?'*
> *For the pagans run after all these things, and your heavenly Father knows that you need them.*
> *But seek first his kingdom and his righteousness, and all these things will be given to you as well.*
> *Therefore do not worry about tomorrow, for tomorrow will worry about itself. Each day has enough trouble of its own."*

The key here, is not to worry. God has a plan to help each one of us get through this, or any other crisis. He understands our basic needs for survival. He has already set His plan in motion to meet those needs. But we must be wise and faithful, and seek Him and His solutions to our needs. We must do all that we can faithfully do, and then let God do what He will faithfully do.

It is important to remember that as God's children we are joint-heirs with Christ (Romans 8:16-17). As members of God's family and coheirs with Christ, we have certain inalienable rights—certain provisions for life here on earth—that God will not take from his children, for the *Father knows that you need them.*

We can, however, lose those provisions if we do not take precautions or make plans to procure them. God provides an abundance of resources for us to enjoy. But He doesn't deliver groceries to our front door. He expects some effort from us. He has given us the wisdom and the skills to either grow our own food, or to earn money so that we can pay someone else for the food we need.

The same way with the Year 2000. God has the answers. He has the resources. But we must seek Him for them. *"Ask and it will be given to you,"* Jesus says, *"seek and you will find; knock and the door will be opened to you. For everyone who asks receives; he who seeks finds; and to him who knocks, the door will be opened"* (Matthew 7:7-8). God does not automatically assume nor desire to violate the will of His children concerning all that He has for them.

"But they [the disciples] *did not understand what he* [Jesus] *meant and were afraid to ask him about it"* (Mark 9:32). It is sometimes hard to receive what you need or desire if you do not ask. Too many Christians are afraid to ask God for anything. Why? Jesus Himself told His followers to "ask," yet we do not. Perhaps it is because we lack the confidence that we are worthy enough to approach God. If we accept that it is only through Christ that we are worthy, and only through Him that we may petition God, then we would feel free to come before God without fear and trembling. Perhaps we are afraid that our request of God will be ignored or rejected. Or perhaps we feel that we are better able to take care of ourselves and meet our own needs. There are undoubtedly a host of reasons why we do not approach God, our heavenly Father, more in relationship to our earthly needs.

Often when we do ask, we do not receive because we ask with the wrong intent, or the wrong desire. In James 4:2-3, the Apostle James wrote: *"You want something but don't get it. You kill and covet, but you cannot have what you want. You quarrel and fight. You do not have, because you do not ask God. When you ask, you do not receive, because you ask with wrong motives, that you may spend what you get on your pleasures."* James is clearly identifying two primary reasons why God's people do not receive from Him. First, rather than asking God they strive to meet their needs by their own dishonorable methods: lust, greed, killing, cheating, fighting, etc. Second, if they do ask God they ask for the wrong things, with wrong motives, just to satisfy their own lusts. When we come before God our desires and motives should be in keeping with Godly intent and biblical principles, and that the blessing we seek is also to enable us to bless others.

The Psalmist David puts forth this great prayer of blessing in Psalm 20:

> *May the LORD answer you when you are in distress; may the name of the God of Jacob protect you.*
> *May he send you help from the sanctuary and grant you support from Zion.*
> *May he remember all your sacrifices and accept your burnt offerings. Selah*
> *May he give you the desire of your heart and make all your plans succeed.*
> *We will shout for joy when you are victorious and will lift up our banners in the name of our God. May the LORD grant all your requests.*
> *Now I know that the LORD saves his anointed; he answers him from his holy heaven with the saving power of his right hand.*
> *Some trust in chariots and some in horses, but we trust in the name of the LORD our God.*
> *They are brought to their knees and fall, but we rise up and stand firm.*
> *O LORD, save the king! Answer us when we call!*

Two things that excite me, and I hope you, that could be a positive result of the Year 2000 dilemma. 1. A greater reliance on God by each one of us. 2. A greater sense of the reality of the Body of Christ on earth—the community of saints in Christ—as well as a greater sense of supportive community among neighbors. The twentieth century has brought us many wonders and technological advances, but at what cost to humanity? Our fast-paced lives and striving for worldly success has torn apart faith, moral values, families, neighborhoods, and basic trust in one another, and in what God can do for each of us together.

God desires to grant the petitions of His children, but we must ask, and ask with honorable intent. In 2 Chronicles 1:7, it is recorded: *"That night God appeared to Solomon and said to him, 'Ask for whatever you want me to give you.'"*

Solomon could have asked God for anything his heart desired. He could have asked for great power, or great wealth, or victory over his enemies, but he did not. Instead, in his desire to be a servant of the people, Solomon said to God: *"Give me wisdom and knowledge, that I may lead this people, for who is able to govern this great people of yours?"* (verse 10). Because Solomon put others before his own gratification, God granted his request but also granted him great wealth, riches, and honor.

As we seek God for wisdom in dealing with the Year 2000 crisis and how we can best prepare, let us also be seeking Him for ways we can help our family, neighbors, community, and brothers and sisters in Christ. Through such selfless desires and requests we will not only find more of God in our lives, but a greater sense of what it means to be in community with our neighbor.

Points to Ponder

List five areas where you need to get your life right with God—NOW!

1. ______________________________

2. ______________________________

3. ______________________________

4. ______________________________

5. ______________________________

List five general areas where you know you are going to need God's help to get through the Year 2000 challenge.

1. ______________________________
2. ______________________________
3. ______________________________
4. ______________________________
5. ______________________________

List five prayer requests that you will petition God for until you receive the answers.

1. ______________________________
2. ______________________________
3. ______________________________
4. ______________________________
5. ______________________________

14

If My People ...

Humble yourselves before the Lord, and he will lift you up.

(James 4:10)

In the midst of a crisis, as in any time in our life, God would like us to think about Him and call upon Him *first*. Too often we get ourselves into difficult spots because we do not seek God first. And there is certainly not a more difficult spot that man has placed himself in than in the midst of the voracious Millennium Bug. It just may be the biggest challenge to face mankind since World War II, or the Great Depression. If nothing else, it is the greatest mobilization of the nation's resources—time, money, and people—in over 50 years.

But this mobilization will not be enough to conquer the Bug. We have still left out the most vital resource we have: God. What does God have to do with all this? God says, *"If my people, who are called by my name, will humble themselves and pray and seek my face and turn from their wicked ways, then will I hear from heaven and will forgive their sin and will heal their land"* (2 Chronicles 7:14). Our founding fathers of the great United States of America chose to call upon God to bless their endeavor in a new land, and to seek His guidance. But, as a nation, and as God's people, we have rebelled against God and rejected His wisdom and truth. To overcome this neglect of God and to give us strength to deal with Y2K, we must enter into a right relationship with God.

Intercession

Before you strike out into the fray of the battle you must have on the whole armor of God: truth, righteousness, gospel of peace, faith, salvation, the word of God, prayer and intercession (Ephesians 6:11-18). Prayer and intercession are first and foremost when it comes to doing battle to seal the breach and stand in the gap. If you are not a prayer warrior, join forces with someone who is one. Paul, in exhorting Timothy, says, "*I urge, then, first of all, that requests, prayers, intercession and thanksgiving be made for everyone*" (1 Timothy 2:1). Scripture says that God is just looking for opportunities to show Himself strong on our behalf (2 Chronicles 16:9), but that He is displeased because He can find no one to intercede on the behalf of men (Isaiah 59:16; 64:7). While Jesus is continually before God as our intercessor (Romans 8:34), God expects us also to intercede for others. Not only are we to pray and intercede on our own, but we are to join forces with the Holy Spirit, Who will intercede with us in accordance with God's will (Romans 8:26-27; Ephesians 6:18).

To intercede means to *mediate*, *plead*, or *pray* on the behalf of others. In addition to Jesus, Moses and Job were two great examples of intercessors. They were continually before God on behalf of the people (Psalms 106:23) or their friends (Job 42:10). Jesus teaches that we are to pray a prayer of faith (Mark 11:24), and tells a parable on how we are to be persistent before God (Luke 18:1-7). Jesus was persistent in prayer (Luke 6:12).

Be faithful, dedicated, single-minded, and disciplined. *"Do not be anxious about anything,"* Paul says, *"but in everything, by prayer and petition, with thanksgiving, present your requests to God"* (Philippians 4:6). When we pray and intercede, we must have the mind of Christ. Jesus instructed that when we pray we are to believe that we have already received what we prayed for (Matthew 21:22; Mark 11:24).

How are we to pray and intercede? With **faith.** With **conviction**. With **expectation**. With **sincerity.** With **passion**. Yes, passion. The Apostle James counsels, *"Therefore confess your sins to each other and pray for each other so that you may be healed. The prayer of a righteous man is powerful and effective"* (James 5:16). The King James version of the Bible translates this prayer as an *"effectual fervent prayer."*

What is a *fervent* prayer? To be fervent, means to be ardent, passionate, earnest, intensely devoted, with great warmth of feeling, burning, and glowing—**HOT!** A prayer of intense emotional involvement. Paul says to pray *"in the Spirit on all occasions with all kinds of prayers and requests. With this in mind, be alert and always keep on praying for all saints"* (Ephesians 6:18).

Confession and Repentance

Confession simply means to acknowledge the sin in our life and admit to our guilt. Repentance, the desired outcome for recognizing our sin, is where we genuinely feel sorry for what we have done or failed to do. *"Then I acknowledged my sin to you,"* David says, *"and did not cover up my iniquity. I said, 'I will confess my transgressions to the Lord'— and you forgave the guilt of my sin"* (Psalm 32:5). In both the Hebrew and Greek languages, the concept of true confession was that it was a form of worship before God—of coming clean before Him, so that one could freely covenant with Him without the barrier of sin. Proverbs 28:13 says, *"He who conceals his sins does not prosper, but whoever confesses and renounces them finds mercy."*

Biblical repentance is not often seen today. In the Old Testament, when the Jews repented, it was a thing of great emotion, regret, and display *"in dust and ashes"* (Job 42:6). In today's world of self and lack of taking responsibility for one's sinful actions, such outward displays of repentance are unheard of, but would certainly be welcomed in some circles. *"Godly sorrow,"* says Paul, *"brings repentance that leads to salvation and leaves no regret, but worldly sorrow brings death"* (2 Corinthians 7:10). Jesus says, that unless we all repent, we will all perish (Luke 13:3).

Forgiveness and Restitution

Forgiveness has three components to it:

1. To know that we are forgiven by God,

2. To know that the ones we have wronged forgive us,

3. To offer forgiveness to those that have wronged us.

It is the last two that are sometimes hard to come by, but the first is readily offered by God through Jesus Christ. When we are forgiven or forgive, it means that we have received, or are offering to someone else, a **pardon**. We are offering, as God has done through the blood of Jesus, to give up resentments, anger, and our desire for retribution against those that have hurt or wronged us. We are, as Jesus has done, canceling the debt we feel others owe us. *"Do not judge,"* Jesus says, *"and you will not be judged. Do not condemn, and you will not be condemned. Forgive, and you will be forgiven"* (Luke 6:37).

While confession, repentance, and forgiveness may not solve your Y2K problems, it will help you be more spiritually and mentally prepared for the Year 2000, or any other challenge that might come your way. It will help you have greater understanding of the nature and power of God and the resources He has for each one of us. King David says, *"Blessed is he whose transgressions are forgiven, whose sins are covered. Blessed is the man whose sin the Lord does not count against him and in whose spirit is no deceit"* (Psalm 32:1-2).

It is much better to enter into a crisis, or in going through life in general, to know that your sins are forgiven, that you are blessed of God, and that He does not hold your transgressions against you. It leaves your mind, spirit, and emotions free to focus on other issues of importance in your life, such as dealing with Year 2000 preparedness issues. *"Be kind and compassionate to one another,"* says the Apostle Paul, *"forgiving each other, just as in Christ God forgave you"* (Ephesians 4:32).

Sometimes repentance and receiving forgiveness may require that we make restitution—give back or restore to the rightful owner that which we stole or destroyed. The attitude we are to have when making restitution is set forth by Zacchaeus in Luke 19. *"But Zacchaeus* [a tax collector] *stood up and said to the Lord, 'Look, Lord! Here and now I give half of my possessions to the poor, and if I have cheated anybody out of anything, I will pay back four times the amount.' Jesus said to him, 'Today salvation has come to this house, because this man, too, is a son of Abraham. For the Son of Man came to seek and to save what was lost'"* (verses 8-10). Zacchaeus' attitude was to restore even more than what he had wrongfully taken, so that the one he wronged would not only have his money restored but be richly blessed at the same time.

Spiritual Warfare

A large part of preparing for the Year 2000 dilemma will be spiritual warfare. Make no mistake about it, the devil will be using every avenue available to deceive God's people and the world by sowing misinformation, lies, a false sense of security, and fear. Families, neighbors, and churches will need to pick up the pace of prayer and intercession. While we may see the battle as technological or human in nature, Paul warns that, *"our struggle is not against flesh and blood, but against the rulers, against the authorities, against the powers of this dark world and against the spiritual forces of evil in the heavenly realms"* (Ephesians 6:12). We must be ever vigilant, and always prayerful.

It is beyond the intent and scope of this chapter and book to present an entire description or study on how to be spiritually prepared for a universal crisis such as Y2K. In addition to the forgoing, others may feel lead to a period of **fasting** as a way to tune in to God's direction for them and others. Most of us may find it necessary and prudent to increase the level of our **faith** and trust in God. Hopefully, many will be lead to personal **sacrifice** to help meet or serve the needs of others in their churches or communities.

To satisfactorily and sufficiently get through this crisis together, we will all need to build our level of faith and trust in God, and **stand on the promises of God.** There is no better way to build our faith and trust than to **worship and praise** Him with **thanksgiving** in our hearts. Perhaps Paul says it best: *"Speak to one another with psalms, hymns and spiritual songs. Sing and make music in your heart to the Lord, always giving thanks to God the Father for everything, in the name of our Lord Jesus Christ"* (Ephesians 5:19-20).

As importantly as any other method of building your faith, do not forget God's Word. Study it and share it. You may even want to memorize certain passages that bring you comfort and peace that you can call upon in times of anxiety or fear over the Year 2000, or anything else that might be challenging you. Above all, know that God is there, call upon Him, and He will answer.

Points to Ponder

List five sins that you know you need to seek God's, and perhaps the forgiveness of others.

1. ____

2. ____

3. ____

4. ____

5. ____

List five ways you could strengthen your faith and reliance on God.

1. ____

2. ____

3. ____

4. ____

5. ____

15

Building Your Hedge

I looked for a man among them who would build up the wall and stand before me in the gap on behalf of the land so I would not have to destroy it, but I found none.
(Ezekiel 22:30)

In your daily walk with the Lord, are you a **gap**-*maker* or a **gap**-*plugger*? Are you a **breach**-*maker* or a **breach**-*repairer*?

In Ezekiel 22:29-30 (KJV), God spoke through the prophet Ezekiel saying, *"The people of the land have used oppression, and exercised robbery, and have vexed the poor and needy: yea, they have oppressed the stranger wrongfully. And* ***I sought for a man*** *among them, that should* ***make up the hedge****, and* ***stand in the gap*** *before me for the land, that I should not destroy it: but* ***I found none"*** (author's emphasis). The Hebrew word for *stand* means to *abide* in, *appoint*, *dwell* in, *endure*, *establish* a position, *raise up*, or *remain* in place.

In our Christian walk there are many opportunities for us to stand in the gap—for our family, our church, our business, our faith. The challenge of Year 2000 is another such opportunity that will test our courage, resolve, and faith. How each one of us chooses to respond will determine our success or failure to meet those challenges. How we respond individually and corporately as the Body of Christ will either be a testimony to His presence in our lives or a detriment to the mission of the Church and the saving grace that Jesus offers everyone. We can chose a response to the issues of Y2K that would cause us not to stand in the gap or build up our hedge of protection; or we can take the initiative as God expects, and take action that will plug the gap of our susceptibility to the impact of Y2K in our lives—at home, at work, at our church, and in our community.

It has been said that Albert Einstein's definition of insanity was doing the same thing over, and over, and over, and expecting the results to be different. For each of us the Year 2000 Bug will have both a direct and indirect impact. It will require that we do some things over, such as exercising faith. But for many of us this will require that we not exercise the level of faith we are accustomed to, but a higher level of faith that will bring better results. If you are the type of person that tends to ignore potential problems, hoping they will go away, or that someone else will solve them for you, then this will require that you not follow the same approach to Y2K. Not being prepared for Year 2000 should not be one of your options. You must build up your hedge of protection in the best way you are able.

Plug the Gap

It is time for us all to be gap-pluggers. To be repairing the Year 2000 breaches in our homes and communities. We must all be willing to tackle the challenge head-on—to climb that mountain of obstacles before us. **It's time to take a stand!** We must stop posturing our defense and go on the offensive against the Y2K bug—for our families, churches, businesses, and communities. This is not an individual problem or challenge, it is a shared problem and experience that will require us all to be up to the challenge: to pray all that we can, to learn all we can about it, and to do all that we can to prepare for it and overcome it.

When January 1, 2000 arrives, none of us will want to be one of whom the Lord could say, *"You have not gone up to the breaks in the wall to repair it for the house of Israel so that it will stand firm in the battle on the day of the Lord"* (Ezekiel 13:5). If you put your family's surname in the place of *Israel*, you will see the importance of that passage.

Now, ask yourself: What haven't I done for my family to stand in the gap and make up a protective hedge around my loved ones? How have I not yet prepared for the impact of the Year 2000—spiritually, materially, financially, emotionally? Have you let down your guard by not interceding for your family, your church, your community, your government, your place of employment, by not becoming a student of the Word of God, by rejecting His covering of Church authority, by turning from the strength of the Body of Christ and the fellowship of believers, by being disobedient to God's word or His calling on your life, by trying to ignore the Y2K issue? Before you can stand in the gap, you must know where the gap exists, and at what point of entry the attacker is breaching your defenses. Before you can make up a hedge, you must know what it is that you are protecting, and what the hedge must be made of to keep the enemy out of your midst. In the case of the Year 2000, the previous chapters clearly identified the problem (or enemy), the points of attack, and where your defenses need to be built.

Stand in the Gap and Build Up Your Hedge—NOW!

The time for Y2K preparedness is *now*. Not next week, next month, or next year, but as soon as you finish reading this book (chapters19-24 gives you specific things you can do to be prepared). *"The Lord will guide you always; he will satisfy your needs in a sun-scorched land and will strengthen your frame. You will be like a well-watered garden, like a spring whose waters never fail. Your people will rebuild the ancient ruins and will raise up the age-old foundations; you will be called Repairer of Broken Walls, Restorer of Streets with Dwellings"* (Isaiah 58:11-12). Now, wouldn't you like to be known by God—and your family, your church, your community—as the "Repairer of Broken Walls," the "Restorer of Streets with Dwellings?" Figuratively speaking, all of us will need to be repairers and restorers in dealing with the potential impact of Y2K. We can choose to sit back and let it happen, and receive any consequences of our inaction, or we can choose to be pro-active and part of the solution—if not in fixing the problem, at least in preparing to lessen its potential negative impact.

Repair the Breach

If we chose to stand in the gap, as well as build up our defenses as a repairer and restorer, then God says He will continually guide us, satisfy our needs, and strengthen us. Also, as a result of this choice we will be a beacon (*a spring*) to those around us, and will be a part of the rebuilding process. The results of Year 2000 preparedness, or lack thereof, will require rebuilding at all levels that affect our lives—family, church, community, work, city services, government, etc.

If we rely on God and the wisdom He gives us, then He will provide spiritual strength and nurture during time of stress and potential lack (*sun-scorched land*). He will prosper our way (*satisfy your needs*). By God's hand we will be a source of plenty (*like a well-watered garden*); a place of refreshment for our families and others (*like a spring whose waters never fail*). Because of our sacrifice and willingness—and that of many others in our churches and communities—to stand in the gap and be repairers and restorers, our families, our fellow church members, our communities, will be able to rebuild the potential wasteland created by the Y2K Bug.

This does not necessarily mean that we will not have to experience or go through the initial impact of Y2K on our lives, our church, our community, or our place of employment. But it does mean that when we experience the impact of Year 2000 glitches, just like any other challenge we may face in our life, God is there. He is with us, and ever ready to guide and strengthen us during times of personal or corporate challenge or roadblocks and show us the way out. But notice, it starts with YOU: *"**You** will be . . . and **you** will be called the Repairer of Broken Walls, the Restorer of Streets with Dwellings."*

Does this mean that God's people will never face trials and tribulations? No. Please note: God says, *"**in** a sun-scorched land" (drought*, KJV). A place that is in a sun-scorched land is called a desert, a very dry place. While going through a tribulation experience, such as Y2K, it may not be pleasant, and one that we would just as soon avoid. The consolation, of sorts, is that we are all going to experience it to varying degrees. How each one of us experiences it will depend on our spiritual, mental, and material preparation. But not only us as individuals. Our success in dealing with Y2K will depend on how well prepared we are as churches, communities, and neighborhoods.

A person who is strong in faith gives glory to God amidst the circumstances of their drought (see Romans 4:19-21). *"Who shall separate us from the love of Christ?"* Paul says. *"Shall trouble or hardship or persecution or famine or nakedness or danger or sword?. . . No, in all these things we are more than conquerors through him who loved us. For I am convinced that neither death nor life, neither angels nor demons, neither the present nor the future, nor any powers, neither height, nor depth, nor anything else in all creation, will be able to separate us from the love of God that is in Christ Jesus our Lord"* (Romans 8:35, 37-39).

Why should we rejoice in the midst of our trials and tribulations and even "consider it pure joy" as the Apostle James says in James 1:2? While we may not like the suffering we are going through, we can rejoice in what we know God can do with us and through us in the midst of the situation, knowing with confidence that if we keep our eyes on Jesus, He will not fail us or forsake us. Keep in mind that suffering, while not of God's doing, is one way that He can mature the fruit of the Spirit within us, which is *"love, joy, peace, patience, kindness, goodness, faithfulness, gentleness and self-control. Against such things there is no law"* (Galatians 5:22-23).

Be a Provider

One more decision must be made before you stand in the gap for your family: You must decide that you want to be a provider for your family, a spiritual head, while meeting the temporal needs of your family. To some, this may seem like a suggestion that does not need to be made, but in today's society many do not want to take responsibility for the spiritual and material needs of their families. It is a decision that all family heads must make before standing in the gap, and particularly in the light of the Year 2000 challenge. If you do not make this decision in favor of your family you may want to heed Paul's directive to family heads—particularly those headed by men. *"If anyone does not provide for his relatives, and especially for his immediate family, he has denied the faith and is worse than an unbeliever"* (1 Timothy 5:8).

The burden of responsibility, Paul says, for providing for one's family, is placed squarely on the shoulders of the head of the household. Not the government, not the church, not your employer, and not your neighbor. However, other able bodied members of a family are not exempt. Adult children, for example, should make sure that their parents are prepared or provided for, and those in our family tree that are not able to adequately prepare. While God expects us to provide for our own, we are also called to reach out to others, and help them meet their needs as well. To keep our individual boats afloat in the oncoming tide of Y2K it will take the combined and cooperative effort of all those we care about and are in association with at the local level.

Abide in Christ

Jesus says: *"Remain in me, and I will remain in you. No branch can bear fruit by itself; it must remain in the vine. Neither can you bear fruit unless you remain in me"* (John 15:4). To remain in or abide in, means to *stand fast with*, to *stay with*, or to *continue with*. For standing in the gap to be a success, you must always abide in Christ, and let Him abide in you. *"If anyone does not remain in me,"* Jesus says, *"he is like a branch that is thrown away and withers; such branches are picked up, thrown into the fire and burned. If you remain in me and my words remain in you, ask whatever you wish, and it will be given you"* (John 15:6,7). How does Jesus abide in us, and we in Him? He abides in us through the presence of the Holy Spirit in us (John 14:16; 1 John 2:27, 3:24). We abide in Him by letting our spiritual self die (John 12:24), through our faith in Him (1 John 2:6), and obedience to His word (1 John 3:6, 24; 2 John 1:9). Now that you abide in Christ, and He in you, you are ready to charge into battle; to stand in the gap.

Points to Ponder

List five breaches (gaps) in your spiritual hedge.

1. ______________________________

2. ______________________________

3. ______________________________

4. ______________________________

5. ______________________________

List five ways that you are going to repair your spiritual hedge.

1. ______________________________

2. ______________________________

3. ______________________________

4. ______________________________

5. ______________________________

List five people who could help you build your spiritual hedge.

1. ______________________________

2. ______________________________

3. ______________________________

4. ______________________________

5. ______________________________

16

Staying In Control (The Caleb Principle)

You will keep in perfect peace him whose mind is steadfast, because he trusts in you.
(Isaiah 26:3)

Are you a plateau-sitter or a mountain-climber? Are you reactive or pro-active? The large majority of people wait for things to happen, while a scant few make things happen. Joshua 14:6-13 gives us a spiritual eye's view of how God expects his people to react during a time of challenge or adversity. These verses reflect the character of Caleb—a man who made things happen.

As recorded in Numbers 13, the Lord told Moses to send twelve Israelites to spy out the Promised Land of Canaan. Of the twelve sent, only two, Joshua and Caleb, then age 40, came back to Moses with a positive report. God had told the Israelites beforehand that the land they were going to was a land *"flowing with milk and honey"* (Exodus 13:5; Joshua 5:6). All twelve spies did agree that it was a fruitful land, literally flowing with milk and honey—but giants possessed the land (Numbers 13:27-28). Although all twelve saw the same things in the Promised Land, and all agreed it was full of riches, ten brought back a negative report of fear about the giants in the land. Why? Because, despite God's promises to the contrary, they could only see obstacles and circumstances. Joshua and Caleb, on the other hand, saw with the eyes of faith, and saw only opportunity and blessing.

After the ten spies got the people riled up with fear of the giants, "*Then Caleb silenced the people before Moses and said, 'We should go up and take possession of the land, for we can certainly do it'*" (Numbers 13:30). Why did Caleb feel this way? Because he had the eyes of faith—he had God's eyes (see Romans 4:17 and 2 Corinthians 4:18). He knew that what God had promised He could deliver. He knew, as Joshua did, that though the land was full of giants, that if God had promised the Israelites that they would possess it, then they were well able to possess it, despite what the outward circumstances looked like.

Are you a Caleb-type Christian? Or are you like one of the ten spies of doubt? In Joshua 14, Caleb is now 85 years old. By today's standards he should be retired or perhaps in a nursing home. Yet he comes before Joshua and says, "*I am still as strong today as the day Moses sent me out; I'm just as vigorous to go out to battle now as I was then*" (Joshua 14:11). This man was no wimp. The King James version says that Caleb was ready "*to go out, and to come in.*" At 85 he was ready to go to war—and he planned on coming back.

Now, Caleb continues, "*give me this hill country* [KJV: *mountain*] *that the LORD promised me that day. You yourself heard then that the Anakims* [the giants] *were there and their cities were large and fortified, but, the LORD helping me, I will drive them out just as he said*" (Joshua 14:12). **Here is a man!** A man who is 85 years old. A man with his prime fighting days far behind him, and he tells Joshua: "*give me this mountain.*" Caleb, an old man, wants the mountain. Not just any mountain, but the mountain where the giants live. A land that the rest of the Israelites saw as only an obstacle to the Promised Land because the cities of the giants were "*large and fortified*."

Caleb was not a plateau-sitter. Caleb was not a man who was ready to take it easy—to sit rocking on the front porch of time. He was not one to turn away from a barrier to his promised land. He was not willing to take what life and circumstances would have given him. He wanted action, and plenty of it. He was not looking for a way out or a way around, but a way into the midst of the challenge. He knew what God had promised— that He would enable the Israelites to possess the Promised Land. He knew what the obstacles were to possessing his portion of it. Instead of faithless fear, his attitude was one of a conqueror, a victor, one who knew the battle had already been won. His attitude was: "Let me get on with it; let me get on with possessing the land, possessing my inheritance." He knew what God had promised, and he knew his God was well able to deliver.

Are you a plateau-sitter? Are you going to get in a stew over the Year 2000 and let the Millennium Bug dictate your response? Or are you going to stand on your foundation of faith and take aggressive action that, with God's help, will secure your future? As a joint-heir with Christ you have already been given the authority to pass through this or any other obstacle. It is time to climb the mountain with the zeal and faith of Caleb. Fear, while it might be your initial motivating emotion, is not an on-going stance for a person of faith. "*The Lord is my light and my salvation*," David proclaims, "*whom shall I fear? The LORD is the stronghold of my life—of whom shall I be afraid?*" (Psalm 27:1).

Slay the Giant

In Deuteronomy 1:21, Moses says, "*See, the LORD your God has given you the land. Go up and take possession of it as the LORD, the God of your fathers, told you. Do not be afraid; do not be discouraged.* " Caleb says, "*Let us go up* ***at once****, and possess* *it; for* ***we are well able to overcome It"*** (Numbers 13:30, KJV, author's emphasis). God had called—no, commanded—the Israelites to go in and possess the Promised Land of Canaan, yet only Caleb and Joshua wanted to go in *at once* and possess what God had already ordained would be theirs.

There is now a perceived and unimaginable giant in the land, called Y2K. We can be fearful and cower at its potential strength, or we can take an active stance of faith and trust in God. As a people, too many have become conditioned to accept what comes their way, often feeling powerless to defend themselves. They become perennial victims, rather than victors. "*Even though I walk through the valley of the shadow of death*," David says, "*I will fear no evil, for you are with me; your rod and your staff, they comfort me"* (Psalm 23:4). King David certainly had a lot to fear in his lifetime. But he kept coming back to his foundation of faith in his sovereign Lord.

God, through the prophet Isaiah, speaks to the House of Israel, as He speaks to each one who accepts Jesus as Lord and Savior: *"Fear not, for I have redeemed you; I have summoned you by name; you are mine. When you pass through the waters, I will be with you; and when you pass through the rivers, they will not sweep over you. When you walk through the fire, you will not be burned; the flames will not set you ablaze. For I am the LORD, your God, the Holy One of Israel, your Savior."*(Isaiah 43:1-3).

While fear might be your initial reaction to this Millennial Bug, you must gain control, and fall back on your foundation in the Millennial Christ. "*For God did not give us a spirit of timidity* [fear], *but a spirit of power, of love and of self-discipline* [a sound mind]" (2 Timothy 1:7). The Apostle John expresses it another way: "*for everyone born of God overcomes the world. This is the victory that has overcome the world, even our faith. Who is it that overcomes the world? Only he who believes that Jesus is the Son of God"* (1 John 5:4,5).

How each one of us reacts, is prepared or unprepared, and overcomes or succumbs to this new millennium obstacle, will be a testimony of our faith and our ability and willingness to trust

God to see us through. While others saw the giants as obstacles to the Promised Land, Caleb chose with the eyes of faith to see them as a challenge that he was well able to meet with God's help. He saw the challenge as a stepping stone and not a stumbling block. Together, with the eyes of faith and God beside us, we too will make it into the promised land of the new millennium.

Points to Ponder

List your best five personal characteristics or traits (handsome or beautiful or other physical traits do not count).

1. ______________________________

2. ______________________________

3. ______________________________

4. ______________________________

5. ______________________________

Name your five weakest character traits.

1. ______________________________

2. ______________________________

3. ______________________________

4. ______________________________

5. ______________________________

List five ways that you have in the past or can stay under control in a crisis.

1. ______________________________

2. ______________________________

3. ______________________________

4. ______________________________

5. ______________________________

List five people you can count on in a crisis that are close in distance.

1. ______________________________

2. ______________________________

3. ______________________________

4. ______________________________

5. ______________________________

17

Equipping The Saints

Again, if the trumpet does not sound a clear call, who will get ready for battle?
(1 Corinthians 14:8)

The Year 2000 crisis and all its tentacles throughout the modern world will be, without question, the greatest modern day challenge to the survival and growth of the Church. If a church and its leadership chooses to ignore this worldly problem, it may not survive. If it chooses to prepare, as well as warn and educate its members, then it will not only survive but become stronger as a result of its wisdom, faithfulness, and testimony. There is no reasonable option for any church, but to warn its members and the community at large. Government has been virtually silent. Business leaders are fearful of future litigation, and are saying nothing of substance. The Church is called of God to instruct the saints and to *prepare God's people for works of service, so that the body of Christ may be built up* (Ephesians 4:12).

Churches Must Come Together for the Good Of All

If there was ever a time for the Christian community to lay aside doctrinal and denominational differences for the good of the whole Body of Christ, now is the time. If the Church does not become pro-active in this issue, many people will panic and suffer needlessly. Those that will be potentially greatly affected by the Y2K disaster—as many experts are calling it—will be those in the cities, the elderly, the poor, the single parent families (particularly those headed by women), and generally, anyone who is not prepared. It is an opportunity for the Church to be bold and take leadership—leadership that is blatantly lacking from the government at any level: local, state, and federal. We, the Church, are called to share with God's people in need (Romans 12:13), and there will be more than the usual number of people in need as a result of Y2K. Let it not be said of your church or the Church at-large: "Where was the Church when all this happened?"

This is a time for all churches to pull together their combined resources—money, materials, information, personnel, and workers—for the good and survival of the whole. Is there such a precedent for cooperative action? Yes.

There are a number of occasions in the Book of Acts and Paul's letters to the churches where he adamantly encouraged or praised a body of believers for their generosity toward other churches that were in need, even though sometimes the believers doing the giving were not well off themselves (2 Corinthians 8:3-4).

In 2 Corinthians 9:1, Paul writes, *"There is no need for me to write to you about this service to the saints."* Why was there no need for Paul to write to the church at Corinth about being generous toward other believers elsewhere? *"For I know your eagerness to help,"* he wrote in verse 2. It must be strongly emphasized that the Year 2000 crisis is NOT a denominational thing. It is NOT a doctrinal thing. It IS a universal problem that will affect everyone who is reliant on today's technology in any way. The degree to which a local church and its members and the community in which it resides will be adversely affected by Y2K will depend in a large measure on the prayer, wisdom, and preparedness of the church's leadership and members.

The Y2K Impact on the Local Church

The impact on the local church will come in several areas. There may also be other areas that are unique to your church or community. This is not meant to be an all-inclusive list.

Operations

The Year 2000 Bug could start affecting the efficiency and reliability of your day-to-day operations in early 1999 or sooner. Depending on the Y2K readiness of your computer systems and those you link up with, as well as other office equipment, you could start to see some unappreciated foul-ups or scrambling of records. Church credit cards that expire in the year 2000 or later may not be accepted at various places. Banking operations may show up with some glitches. In addition to making sure that any church computers are Y2K compliant, you need to check for any embedded chip problems in office equipment, mechanical systems (heating, air conditioning, elevators, etc.), or anything else you think might be suspect.

Members

All church members, including sometime attendees, will need special guidance and spiritual input to help them through this time.

This will be particularly true of those most vulnerable to any abrupt or unanticipated change in their life: seniors, those with special needs, single parent families, widows, children, those with minimal financial resources, etc. The leaders of the church will have to do just that: LEAD. They will have to become informed and stay spiritually strong so that they can effectively educate and advise the congregation. The foundation of faith of the members will have to be built daily, drawing upon the strength and unity of the entire church body. The more informed and the more prepared church members are, the less they will panic and the less they will suffer.

Missions

A church that supports missions or missionaries has a responsibility to educate and keep them informed about Y2K if their home base is not doing so. It also has an obligation to continue its support, but may want to prayerfully consider taking on new projects requiring a higher level of financial commitment that it may not be able to maintain if Year 2000 negatively impacts its financial resources.

Preaching & Teaching

The level of informed preaching and teaching on the Year 2000 problem will be crucial in building up individuals and the entire congregation. Of primary importance, along with Y2K education, will be faith-building sermons and teaching, as well as encouraging groups of prayer warriors and intercessors that can engage in spiritual warfare, because the devil will use this opportunity to try and tear churches and communities apart. The preaching and teaching should also focus on the nature of community-building within the church, as well as in each neighborhood. The time may come when the local church may have to revert to the New Testament church of Acts 2:42+ (see also Acts 4:32+).

Income from Giving

In the midst of crisis, the concerns of those who normally tithe or give offerings and financially support their local church may quickly turn more to family and self-preservation, an act supported by God and the Bible (see Matthew 12:1-4; 1 Samuel 21:6). If the income drops substantially, will the church be able to maintain its staff and programs of service? If the church currently has a cash flow that exceeds its needs, it should start building a reserve that may have to be relied on to provide vital services, such as food, clothing, and shelter. According to many experts there is a real possibility that many people will be laid off or lose their jobs permanently due to the cause and fallout of Y2K, and other economic impacts.

Trust Funds

Many churches have endowment or trust funds that were established over the years. These should be closely scrutinized and assets perhaps moved to safer havens—if any can exist in the economic and monetary scenarios that some forecast. At bare minimum the church's financial committee or advisors should consider diversifying asset bases throughout more than one financial institution. In the worst case scenario, however, which many Y2K experts believe can and will happen, no financial institution may be absolutely safe.

Resources

All the resources of the church may be under exceptional pressure. More than likely its resources will be stretched and will have to meet many, often exceptional needs. The Acts 2 church mentioned previously may be one way for churches to meet the needs of their members and the local community. Sharing of personal resources should be encouraged by the church leadership during such a crisis. Everyone will have to pull together and pool their skills and resources for the survival of the church and community. To get everyone involved in supporting one another, the church may want to establish a church-wide—or encourage a community-wide—barter system or church (community) dollars (See chapter 24, as well as Addendum 6 of Other Important Resources)

Maintaining Order & Peace

The church and its biblical teaching, and the comfort and support that it can provide can be a major source of calm and peace in the midst of turmoil. Jesus says, *"Peace I leave with you; my peace I give you. I do not give to you as the world gives. Do not let your hearts be troubled and do not be afraid"* (John 14:27). While Jesus is our ultimate source of peace, He also expects us and the Church to be a source of peace for each other. It will have a calming effect and be a source of peace if the entire membership of the Church is pulling together for the good of all. This will be extremely important in light of the real possibility of martial law throughout the land. This is being openly discussed and planned by the White House and the President has signed numerous Executive Orders since mid-1996, as well as Presidential Decision Directive 63 on May 22, 1998, giving him the power to declare martial law if Year 2000 chaos develops. (See chapter 8 for a brief discussion on martial law, and Addendum 7 for the full text of Presidential Decision Directive 63).

Points to Ponder

List five skills that you could use to barter for items or services that you might need in a crisis.

1. ______________________________

2. ______________________________

3. ______________________________

4. ______________________________

5. ______________________________

List five things that you have in excess—more than you really need—that you would be willing to part with to help others in your church or community.

1. ______________________________

2. ______________________________

3. ______________________________

4. ______________________________

5. ______________________________

List five ways that you could help your church or community to get better prepared for the Year 2000 crisis.

1. ______________________________

2. ______________________________

3. ____

4. ____

5. ____

18

The Harvest Is Ripe

"Do you not say, 'Four months more and then the harvest?' I tell you, open your eyes and look at the fields! They are ripe for harvest."
(John 4:35)

There has probably never been an event like Y2K, other than the Great Flood of the Bible, that will adversely affect so great a number of people throughout the world at the same time. If the Church focuses on the problem of Year 2000 entirely, it will get bogged down in fear, and become complacent or immobile. The Church has no viable option on this issue. It must take a stand. It must be a beacon to all who need to see a light on the hill, a beacon of hope. The Church, like the often sleeping giant that it is, must cease its slumber and heed the wake up call.

"He who gathers crops in summer is a wise son, but he who sleeps during harvest is a disgraceful son" (Proverbs

10:5). This will be the greatest opportunity there has ever been in modern times for the harvesting of souls for Christ. The Church CANNOT miss it. Many in the world will be frantic, some destitute, some turning to anything or any method they can to survive. All will be looking for someone or something to give them a safe harbor, a place to moor their rapidly sinking ship. The Church of our Lord Jesus Christ must not only be the lighthouse that points the way to safe harbor, it must also be ready to provide sustenance and peace in the midst of the storm.

The prophet Hosea said, *"for you, Judah, a harvest is appointed"* (Hosea 6:11a). For the Church, a harvest is NOW appointed. The harvest is ripe. But is the Church ready to swing the sickle? The churches, leadership, and members that are taking the Year 2000 dilemma seriously, and preparing themselves, will be ready to harvest the many souls that God sends their way. They will be a beacon to the lost, a testimony of peace and sanity amidst confusion, chaos, and suffering. Will your church be there? Will it sign on to be a light in the midst of darkness, or will it be a part of the darkness, indistinguishable from the doom and gloom that surrounds it?

Jesus said:

> *"But understand this: If the owner of the house had known at what hour the thief was coming, he would not have let his house be broken into. You also must be ready, because the Son of Man will come at an hour when you do not expect him."*
>
> (Luke 12:39-40)

The thief is coming, and he is coming for sure. But unlike this Scripture, where his arrival cannot be timed, the Y2K thief is on a precise schedule and will arrive on time. We *must be ready*, as Jesus says. This thief will steal from all, indiscriminately. While we will not be able to stop its coming, we can prepare to minimize its damage.

The Church must have the heart and compassion of Jesus, Who, *"When he saw the crowds, he had compassion on them, because they were harassed and helpless, like sheep without a shepherd. Then he said to his disciples, 'The harvest is plentiful but the workers are few. Ask the Lord of the harvest, therefore, to send out workers into his harvest field'"* (Matthew 9:36-38).

Y2K has the potential to impact people's lives to the point where they have no control over their situations and circumstances. Especially if they are inadequately prepared for it. With the potential of limited or no utilities, a collapsed economy and monetary system, unemployment, minimal government services, and the looming potential of martial law, many people will become frustrated, angry, depressed, and possibly out of control. Particularly, if severe conditions drag on for more than a month in what will be winter in many parts of the world. The Church must be ready and willing to lead the lost and confused with the love and compassion of a shepherd. God did not create this rapidly unfolding tragedy, but if we are willing to be His servants He can use it to draw the lost to Christ. *"For God did not appoint us to suffer wrath but to receive salvation through our Lord Jesus Christ. He died for us so that, whether we are awake or asleep, we may live together with him. Therefore encourage one another and build each other up, just as in fact you are doing"* (1 Thessalonians 5:9-11).

In Psalm 133:1, David says, *"How good and pleasant it is when brothers live together in unity!"* The Hebrew for *brothers* or *brethren*, means those that are of the same kindred, kind, or class. In the New Testament we are taught that all those who called upon the name of the Lord and accepted His work of salvation are brothers and sisters in the Lord. The Year 2000 and its many assorted challenges will give the members of local churches a real test and opportunity to demonstrate their love for one another, and for the community of souls that surround them. The Church has such an incredible opportunity to display the self-sacrifice agape love of Christ.

Jesus does not suggest that we love one another, He **commands** it: *"This is my command: Love each other"* (John 15:17). "*A new command I give you: Love one another. As I have loved you, so you must love one another. By this all men will know that you are my disciples, if you love one another* (John 13:34-35). The Church will be on the frontline during the Y2K meltdown. The world will be watching for its response and leadership. Will it be up to the test? Some feel it failed the last big test prior to and during World War II, when much of the world's Christian population sat idle as millions of God's people were imprisoned or slaughtered. Will it be different this time?

The Apostle Paul says that Christ *"gave gifts to men"* (Ephesians 4:8), some of which are apostles, prophets, evangelists, pastors, and teachers *"to prepare God's people for works of service, so that the body of Christ may be built up until we all reach the unity in the faith and in the knowledge of the Son of God and become mature, attaining to the whole measure of the fullness of Christ"* (Ephesians 4:11-13). What a testimony to the world in the midst of crisis for God's people to take the lead, to show the way with *works of service*, building up the *body of Christ* with *unity in the faith*, for the maturing of the saints so that we may know and attain the full measure of Christ.

The inspired apostle Paul wrote:

> *I urge you to live a life worthy of the calling you have received.*
> *Be completely humble and gentle; be patient, bearing with one another in love.*
> *Make every effort to keep the unity of the Spirit through the bond of peace.*
> *There is one body and one Spirit—just as you were called to one hope when you were called—*

> *one Lord, one faith, one baptism; one God and Father of all, who is over all and through all and in all*
>
> (Ephesians 4:1-6).

In John's gospel it's recorded that Jesus prayed:

> *My prayer is not for them* [His disciples] *alone. I pray also for those who will believe in me through their message,*
> *that all of them may be one, Father, just as you are in me and I am in you. May they also be in us so that the world may believe that you have sent me.*
> *I have given them the glory that you gave me, that they may be one as we are one.*
> *I in them and you in me. May they be brought to complete unity to let the world know that you sent me and have loved them even as you have loved me.*
> *Father, I want those you have given me to be with me where I am, and to see my glory, the glory you have given me because you loved me before the creation of the world.*
> *Righteous Father, though the world does not know you, I know you, and they know that you have sent me.*
> *I have made you known to them, and will continue to make you known in order that the love you have for me may be in them and that I myself may be in them.*
>
> (John 17:20-26)

Let it not be said of the Church that it was not worthy or ready for the call—the call to draw a world in chaos to Christ. God is awaiting our response to this great and grand opportunity.

Points to Ponder

List five ways or areas that your church currently has or could have evangelical outreach within your community during the Y2K crisis.

1. ______________________________

2. ______________________________

3. ______________________________

4. ______________________________

5. ______________________________

What spiritual gifts or talents do you have that would be helpful to your church's evangelical outreach?

1. ______________________________

2. ______________________________

3. ______________________________

4. ______________________________

5. ______________________________

19

Seek, And You Will Find

I will instruct you and teach you in the way you should go; I will counsel you and watch over you.

(Psalm 32:8)

Getting good, solid, information about Y2K and its potential impact is one of the best ways to prepare. Helping you to obtain that information is the main purpose of this book, and the focus of this chapter.

Seeking information

Jesus encourages all His followers to ask, seek, and knock. It will take a lot of that on your part and others to find out where your church, community, and place of employment stand for Year 2000 preparedness. You will encounter some problems as you seek information from government officials and politicians—whether local, state, or federal—service providers like hospitals and utilities, and virtually all industry areas of employment. You must be well informed on the Y2K issue so that you know what questions to ask, and to be able to judge the quality and truthfulness of the responses. One of the most ambiguous responses that you will get, and one that you must be prepared to press past to get a specific answer, is "We're working on it."

A major part of the Year 2000 problem is misinformation, or no information of substance. Remember, the federal government probably knew about this problem as early as 1969, but did nothing. The President, despite widespread knowledge of the impending problem in the computing industry, did not take any action until February 4, 1998, with the signing of his Executive Order to create a White House Council to head up the government's Y2K effort. Except for an address on July 14, 1998 before the National Academy of Sciences, neither the President nor any member of his staff have addressed or warned the general public on the issue as of this date, October 1998. In addition, few state governments have presented anything to their residents on the status of their Year 2000 readiness. So, don't expect much straight forward information from government officials at any level on this matter of Y2K preparedness.

For the most part, the public service sector and private industry are afraid to say anything other than make general, non-committal, statements on their Y2K efforts or status because they believe they might leave themselves open to future lawsuits. The SEC (Securities Exchange Commission) and other regulatory agencies are having a tough time finding out just how prepared the private and public sectors are as a result of the business's or entity's lack of disclosure. Seeking out information and putting demands on public officials, community and industry leaders, is not only worth the effort, but it is imperative that you get accurate and honest disclosure. Obviously this is a big task for any one person, so you may have to organize your neighborhood or community into task forces (see chapter 24).

Areas You Should Be Concerned About

When it comes to being prepared for the Year 2000 on a community-wide basis, assuming you have an adequate place to live, you need to be seeking information on vital community services. These include water, power, heat, food, transportation (public, but also including snow removal, etc.), medical services, governmental services (city, county, and state), financial services (banking, credit union, investment, lending), sanitation (sewer, septic service, waste removal), communication (telephone, including cellular, pagers, radio, and TV), and emergency services (police, fire, and ambulance).

As you seek information and ask questions, keep in mind that the Y2K battle is on several fronts, and you must cover them all to get a complete and accurate assessment. There is the much publicized computer problem. But of equal importance, is the embedded chip (also known as microchip or silicon) problem. When you talk about computer compliance you must also ask about the Y2K compliance of vendors and suppliers. Then there is the integration of systems. How is the company or other entity doing on integrating their Year 2000 compliance progress with other critical computer systems in other departments, across other companies and networks, and with government agencies or foreign companies, if that is a critical link to their business? Then there is a whole host of related issues that affect all enterprises, such as utilities and other community support services. Of course, you will want to inquire also of their contingency plans in case their computers go down, or utilities are unavailable, etc. What are they going to do in case things fail to work?

Examples of Questions for Various Utility Companies

Let's say you wanted to know how a local utility company is coming on its Y2K preparedness, what would you ask them to get the information you need? Following are a series of possible, but not necessarily all inclusive, questions you might want to get answers to, and not in any particular order of priority.

- Who is responsible for the utility company's Y2K project? What is his or her qualifications? Do they have any computer science or programming experience?

- **Comment**—Many smaller utilities may have to rely on in house personnel to coordinate their effort. While not necessarily bad, it may not give the best talent to deal with the problem. Larger utilities should have hired an outside Y2K expert or consulting firm with Y2K experience.

- When did they first start looking into their Y2K problem?

- **Comment**—If your utility was not in full swing on their Year 2000 project by early 1998—or considerably earlier for large utility companies, you should be concerned about their ability to make the compliance deadline.

- Are they using any outside Year 2000 consultants? If so, who are they and how often are they on site to help them work through the process?

- **Comment**—With outside consultants it would be helpful to know their credentials, other clients, and how much Y2K experience they or their firm has to offer.

- How many people in the company are working on the Y2K problem and how many people hours per week are being spent to address the problem? Are they handling the problem totally with in-house personnel?

- **Comment**—From these two answers you should be able to get a sense as to the priority the utility management and board are placing on this problem, and that it is not just a token effort.

- At this point, are they looking to completely solve the problem through fixes, replacements, and system retirements, or will patch kits be used?

- **Comment**—The utility company, just like any other entity, should only be looking at fixing (re-coding), replacing, or retiring affected systems. If they are looking for patch-ups or patch kits, they are only taking a Band-Aid approach to buy time, but could be jeopardizing the community and any long term solution to the Y2K problem.

- At what stage are they in their Y2K process? Developing a plan of action? Assessment of potential computers or embedded systems that could be affected? Re-coding/fix-up? Testing? Trouble shooting? Re-testing? Integrated system testing?

- **Comment**—If your utility is only in the planning or assessment stage, or is not scheduled for a full test by late 1998 or sooner, it's time to buy candles and prepare for emergency heating if you live in a cold winter climate.

- When are they scheduled to do a system-wide test? Or, if they have tested already, what was the result?

- **Comment**—The sooner the utility gets the first test behind it, the sooner it can trouble shoot and re-test. Keep in mind that in general utility companies across America are running way behind schedule.

- What types of embedded microchip systems are they checking out for Y2K compliance?

- **Comment**—Embedded chips with potential Y2K problems could be associated with telephone systems, certain machinery, pumping stations, switches that control power flow, etc.

- Where do they get their electricity and natural gas from? Do they have written certification that their suppliers are or will be Y2K compliant?

- **Comment**—Most utility companies today do not exist in a vacuum of their own, but rely on other suppliers for their electric and gas. It is extremely important that these suppliers are Y2K compliant.

- Can they generate any of their own electricity? For how long? Can they supply all the community's electricity needs?

- **Comment—**You want to make sure that the company can supply more than just a supplemental amount of electricity, or only for short periods.

- If for some reason their best efforts to prepare for the Year 2000 fall short, what are their contingency plans to meet the community's needs?

- **Comment—**Not having a contingency plan is not acceptable. You will want to get specific details of any contingency plan.

- If a water or sewage plant, how will they pump water without electricity.

- **Comment—**These are crucial concerns that need answers. Not only for personal needs, but for fire fighting, medical services, and the operation of many manufacturing concerns.

- How do they plan to keep the public informed of their Y2K progress? Are they recommending families prepare for alternative means of replacing their vital services in case of failure?

- **Comment**—The utility company and any other vital service in the community should be up front with reporting to the public and progress or delay in meeting Year 2000 deadlines. In the case of the vital services of utilities, responsible leadership should be advising the community on alternatives in case of utility failure—after all it will be January and cold in many parts of the country. A simple "don't worry, we'll make it" or "we're confident everything will be okay" just won't cut it when it comes to people's lives, safety, and comfort.

- When will they be doing integrated testing with their electric and natural gas suppliers?

- **Comment—**Integrated testing is critical. If your local utility is compliant but its suppliers are not, it will not do **you** any good.

- How many critical non-utility-supplying vendors do they rely on? For what services? Do they have certification that the vendors are or will be compliant?

- **Comment**—It is highly unlikely that all vendors will make the deadline, but it is important to know the status of the ones that provide critical services or supplies.

- When does the utility company's fiscal year 2000 start?

- **Comment—**The fiscal year 2000 is the real deadline for the utility company to be compliant, not December 31, 1999.

There will be more questions that you can ask, so don't feel limited to these. You can use similar questions and add appropriate other questions for your local government, law enforcement, emergency services, hospital, sanitation, road department, place of employment, etc. Think about what vital service the organization supplies that you count on, and what you would do without it, to help you draft questions that need answers. You may want to enlist other community members to draft a combined questionnaire and then seek to publish the results in your local newspaper as a community service.

You will want to know the exact **contingency plans** of every vital service in your community. In addition to similar questions for critical services like medical, law enforcement, fire department, and emergency ambulance service, you will want to know what their emergency back-up power system is and how long they can operate at reasonable capacity on that system. You will also want to know if their emergency equipment and communications systems are or will be Year 2000 compliant. For hospitals and medical care facilities you should ask what their back-up heating source is or how they would plan on keeping their facilities warm if there was no electric or natural gas supply for more than a brief period.

With law enforcement (local, county, and state) it would be important to know if they have a riot control plan and what it is (if they will divulge it). Are they checking their electronic jail locks for Y2K flaws. If there is no power or telephone, how could you reach them in an emergency—CB or ham radio? Ask your local governing body if their traffic control and road maintenance systems will be Y2K compliant and what contingency plans they have for snow removal, etc. It would also be helpful to know what plans your local Civil Defense and Red Cross organizations have in the case of emergency situations.

For more considerations on personal and community preparation, see chapters 23 and 24.

Points to Ponder

List five people you know in your community who are directly working on a Year 2000 project in your community or close by.

1. ______________________________
2. ______________________________
3. ______________________________
4. ______________________________
5. ______________________________

List five major employers in your community area.

1. ______________________________
2. ______________________________
3. ______________________________
4. ______________________________
5. ______________________________

List five employers that are dependent on sources outside your community for their supplies, services, or product sales.

1. ______________________________
2. ______________________________

3. ____

4. ____

5. ____

Disclaimer. This chapter, as well as the entire book, is designed to provide general information in regard to the subject matter being covered. It is provided with the understanding that neither the author nor the publisher is engaged in rendering legal, medical, financial, or other professional services through this publication. It should not be used as a substitute for professional legal, medical, financial, technical advice or services if a professional is required.

20

GIVE YOUR PC THE BOOT (UP)

NOTE: For your convenience, here is the Small Business Administration's (SBA's) Y2K Checklists for Small Business. Other helpful Year 2000 information put together by the SBA can be obtained at their Web site: **www.sba.gov/y2k.** Addendum 2 contains addresses of other helpful Y2K Web sites.

Y2K Checklists for Small Business

No single Y2K checklist fits everyone's needs since businesses have a wide variety of services and technologies. The SBA offers several that focus on small business needs, starting with the one below from the Federal Reserve Board. Links to additional checklists, definitions, and resources are provided as well (see also addenda 3, 4, and 5). The SBA says their web site is a "work in progress" and will grow as they come across more information. Keep in mind, there are many excellent checklists on the Internet. Browse the Internet and if you find one you like let the SBA know.

Suggested Steps for Readiness

The most important step is to develop a strategy to make your business ready for the year 2000. Many consulting firms have developed different strategies with 3 to 15 steps to take to help companies deal with the year 2000 problem. Information about these different plans can be found on the Internet or in trade journals. Following is the SBA's simple five-step plan to achieve year 2000 readiness.

1. Awareness—educating and involving all levels of your organization in solving the problem.

A crucial step in awareness is creating a communication strategy to make certain that everyone is informed and that management has the information it needs to make decisions. Holding seminars or meetings to educate people and bringing in outside speakers are two ways to increase awareness.

A critical aspect of awareness is to develop an internal standard for year 2000 readiness. The Federal Reserve uses the following definition: "Systems (e.g., software, hardware, firmware) are defined as ready if they can demonstrate correct management and manipulation of data involving dates, including single-century and multi-century formulas, without causing an abnormally ended scenario within the system or generating incorrect values involving such dates."

The awareness phase never ends. As people move to other jobs, and new people are hired, they must be educated. There is also an ongoing need to keep your staff and business partners informed.

2. Inventory—creating your checklist toward year 2000 readiness.

In this phase, you should identify and list all of the different computer-based systems, components (such as in-house developed systems, purchased software, computers and associated hardware), service providers, and hardware that contain microchips that support your business. Each entry on your list should be ranked by how critical it is to your business.

Indicate in your inventory whether the component is hardware, software, or a service. It may be useful to note which components support your telephone or data communications networks. If a computer-based system uses a vendor-supplied package, record the name of the vendor and the release number, if known.

Hints: Keeping your inventory on a spreadsheet or database makes it easier to sort and report on items that are not ready. It is also helpful to develop an identification system to help track components. For each item on the inventory, assign a person who will be responsible for assessing that item and preparing for the year 2000.

Reminder: Some systems will begin failing before the century date changes because they perform forecasting or future processing. This is called "time horizon to failure," and should be considered during inventory and assessment. The "time horizon to failure" should be listed on your inventory if it is known.

3. Assessment—examining how severe and widespread the problem is in your business and what needs to be fixed.

Starting with the most critical items on the inventory, determine which systems are date-sensitive and if they will fail when the century changes. Systems with an imminent "time horizon to failure" should also be assessed first. A date-sensitive system is one that manipulates or works with dates in some way, or a system that operates differently based upon the date. (Addendum 3 contains questions to help you assess your system's readiness.)

Examples of date-sensitive systems include ones that perform any kind of forecasting or projections through time, such as calculating interest on a loan or projecting inventory levels. Other examples of date-sensitive systems are those that retrieve records based on a date (such as invoices), or systems that sort items by date (such as accounting or inventory systems). Examples of date-sensitive hardware include lighting systems that switch on automatically on weekends, manufacturing control systems, and scanners or card readers that read ID badges or credit/debit cards.

One way to assess a system is to look at the computer code and follow the logic. If this is not possible because the system is based on a purchased package, you should contact the vendor.

Another way to assess a system is to run it as if it were already the year 2000. Running the system with dates other than the current date may require resetting the system date. There are **risks** involved in resetting system dates. Each organization should evaluate the impact of resetting system dates. This testing may require that your test data be "aged" properly so it contains the correct internal dates.

Hint: There are risks involved in rolling the dates on your computer systems forward. Make sure you understand what these risks are for your organization.

For some specialized systems, such as building or manufacturing control systems, or systems with embedded microchips, you may need to have the vendor work with your staff to test and assess the system.

Once you have determined the state of readiness for each system and component listed in your inventory, you should develop a strategy for dealing with those systems that have to be fixed. There are only three possible strategies: repair, replace, or retire the system.

If you decide to **repair** a system, there are two possible repair strategies or approaches: windowing or date expansion. The **date expansion strategy** involves expanding all 2-digit year fields in your system's data files and in the programs that process those files so they can hold the century as well as the 2-digit year. For example, a two-digit year field YY might be expanded to a four-digit CCYY field, where CC is the century. The date expansion may involve increasing the size of files that hold your data.

The **windowing approach** involves inserting logic into your programs that interprets year fields to determine what century the year falls into before the date field is used in calculations, comparisons or sorting. An example of this logic: If the year is between 00 and 49, the century is 20, otherwise the century is 19. This is called the 50 year window. There are other windows. You need to determine which one is appropriate for your particular system. Whatever windowing logic is selected, SBA recommends consistency throughout your organization to avoid later errors and confusion.

Most businesses are taking a mixed approach, fixing some systems using windowing logic and others with date expansion. Some are using a mixed approach to fix even large systems. Your choice depends on your own individual needs.

If your strategy is to **replace** a non-ready system, you have several choices. You can build the replacement in-house (or hire contractors to work with your staff to build it), you can purchase a replacement system from a vendor, or you can outsource that particular line of business to a service bureau or other outside service provider. It is extremely important to determine when the replacement will be ready. If the replacement won't be tested and installed until after the "time horizon to failure," you may be forced into a repair strategy.

A business system that operates in isolation is very rare. Most interface with other business systems to exchange data, and some interface with systems outside your organization. Your strategy to replace or repair non-ready systems should take into account those systems' interfaces with other systems, both within and outside your organization. For example, if you opt for gate expansion, you must consider the impact of sending larger files to all interfaces. If you opt for windowing, all interfaces must be informed what the windowing scheme is.

Hint: SBA recommends that you develop a chart that shows the systems that have interfaces, what those interfaces are, and when they occur.

Different systems that interface with each other may have different schedules for assessment, correction, and implementation. It may be necessary to build bridges between systems that are ready for the year 2000 and those that are not.

These bridges, which are usually temporary programs, take data from one system and modify it to make the format correct for the interfacing system. Careful, detailed, planning will be required to handle these situations.

When you find that a system is not year 2000 ready, determine how critical that system is to your business. For example, if the system prints an invalid date on an internally used report, you may decide that this problem is not significant enough to address. If, however, the system loses track of inventory data or fails to forecast properly, it should be fixed.

Hint: As you purchase new computers, packages, and other hardware, upgrade existing packages, and develop new lines of business, remember that this new equipment needs to be checked to ensure it is year 2000 ready. Upgraded packages also need to be checked for readiness after upgrading.

4. Correction and Testing—implementing the readiness strategy you have chosen and testing the fix.

Testing is a critical aspect of any year 2000 project. Testing verifies that the repaired or replaced system operates properly when the date changes and that existing business functions (such as accounting, inventory control, and order tracking) continue to operate as expected. Testing also verifies that interfacing systems are not adversely affected. You should not confine your testing efforts solely to computer programs. Other systems (including network operating systems, vendor-supplied software, building infrastructure systems, PCs, and components with embedded microchips) should be tested to ensure they will not fail when the century changes.

There are several critical tests you should perform once you've changed or replaced a system. The best way to see if a system is ready for the year 2000 is to test the system as if it were already the year 2000. Test that the system will operate correctly after the date has rolled over from 12/31/1999 to 1/1/2000. Because the year 2000 is a leap year, you should test that your system will recognize 2/29/2000 as a valid date and that it will roll over from

2/28/2000 to 2/29/2000, and from 2/29/2000 to 3/1/2000. You should also test your fixed system with a date before 2000 to ensure that it works (see Addenda 3 and 5 for additional testing information).

Warning: There are **risks** involved in rolling dates forward on computers. Some computer security systems keep track of the last time a user accessed a system and will revoke or inactivate that user's password if it has not accessed the system for a period of time. Rolling the date forward may cause user passwords to be inactivated by the security system. Data-sets that should be retained may be marked as expired and could be written over. Some software packages may be leased and you may be paying an annual fee to the vendor. Rolling the date past the end of the lease may cause the software package to freeze up or generate error messages.

There are several other tests that you may want to carry out, depending on the functions your system supports. If your system does end-of-week, end-of-month, end-of-quarter and/or end-of-year processing, these should be tested. You should test that the system will forecast and retrieve data properly. Set the date to a date in 1999 and check that the system will forecast into the next century. Set the system to a date in the 21st century (any date after 12/31/1999) and test that the system will retrieve historical data from some period before 12/31/1999.

Hint: Whenever possible, testing should be carried out in a test environment to minimize the chance of corrupting the production systems. Also, be careful changing historical or backup files if you choose date expansion. You may lose an important audit trail. SBA suggests you consult with your auditors and legal staff before changing historical or backup files.

Definition: The term "production environment" refers to the set of hardware and software that supports your day-to-day operations. "Test environment" refers to the hardware and software where new or changed systems can be tested without disturbing your day-to-day operations.

Hint: Testing of changed systems should be carried out in an environment that is ready for the year 2000. You should work with your vendors to determine when their hardware platforms will be compliant and use those dates to build your test plans. If your vendor cannot supply the platform in time to meet your schedule, you should be aware of the risks involved and be prepared to retest your changed systems once the platform is ready.

5. Implementation—moving your repaired or replaced system into your production environment.

Before you install your replacement or repaired system, you should develop an installation plan and contingency plans. The installation plan lists all the files and programs that need to be moved into production, and all the steps to make your changed system work. Your installation plan may include testing in production to insure that the installed systems are working as expected. Contingency plans list the possible problems that you can foresee and what steps you will take if these problems occur.

Hint: You may want to make backups of the production files from the old system. If possible, you may want to install the ready system and run it in parallel with the old system and compare results.

Reminder: Your contingency plans should not include reverting to the old system. The old system is not ready for the year 2000, otherwise you would not be replacing or repairing it.

Warning: In planning to replace a system, make certain that you allow enough time to replace all of the necessary pieces of that system.

6. Don't get contaminated

Once you have repaired your systems and made them year 2000 compliant, you should take steps to make sure that subsequent changes do not contaminate those systems with year 2000 bugs.

A system might get contaminated if a programmer makes changes to a repaired system and inadvertently changes the logic that handles the century change. A vendor-supplied package might also become contaminated if subsequent releases of the package don't include the year 2000 changes.

Retest the year 2000 changes as part of any subsequent system modification effort. SBA recommends that you save the test data and test cases that were used to test the original changes and use them whenever you are testing other changes to that system. This is called *regression testing.* They suggest that any new releases of vendor-supplied packages also be year 2000 tested.

7. Personal computers (see Addenda 3 and 4)

Today, personal computers are widely used in many businesses. All personal computers have an internal clock/calendar that maintains and reports the date and time. In some computers, the year is stored and processed as two rather than four digits. The year 2000 will affect these computers just as it affects other systems. If you are running systems on your computers that access that PC's date, these systems may fail or produce bad results. All PCs should be tested, regardless of how they are used.

See Addendum 3 for steps you can follow to test your personal computer. You can also run PC test software that is available on the Internet. One such Internet site is, www.rightime.com/default.htm, which will check your system's BIOS (Basic Input/Output System) for year 2000 compliance.

Take an organized approach to this problem. List all your PCs, test them for readiness, and mark those that are not ready for later attention. Bright fluorescent labels can be used to mark PCs as ready or not.

There are several possible ways to correct this PC date problem. You may contact a computer retailer to investigate purchasing a new BIOS chip that is year 2000 compliant ready, download software solutions from the Internet, or replace the non-ready PC with a model that is.

Hint: Anytime you reset the date on a PC, you run the risk of corrupting your system. You can minimize that risk either by backing up all of the critical files or by resetting the date in a test environment. Don't forget to reset the date to the correct date/time after you have tested the system. If you are testing a LAN file server, power off all of the workstations connected to that LAN before going through the date test procedure.

Warning: Even a brand-new state-of-the-art PC may not be ready for the year 2000. New PCs should be tested before they are installed.

8. Your business is NOT alone

No business exists in a vacuum. Yours is part of a chain of customers, suppliers, utilities, and vendors. Year 2000 failures in any of these can impact your business. Here are some tips to protect your business within this chain.

- **Vendor-supplied products**—Many software vendors were caught by surprise by the year 2000 problem and some will not be able to make their products ready. Others may make their products ready but may not be able to deliver the ready software until late 1999. Some vendors may no longer support a particular product that you may be running, and other vendors may have gone out of business. For date-sensitive systems, contact the vendors to find out their readiness plans. If a vendor will not give you information about the readiness status of a package, or if a ready version will not be available until late in 1999, you should investigate an alternate system. Even if a vendor insists its product can handle the century date change, you still should test and certify it to your satisfaction. If the vendor insists that an upgraded version of a program package is ready, that package still must be tested since the vendor may have a different definition of readiness.

- **Data processing service bureaus**—If you use a service bureau for your data processing needs, contact it to discuss its plans for year 2000 readiness.
  Make a list of all the services provided by your service bureau, ranking them according to how critical they are to your business, and then contact the service bureau in writing about each service. If a service bureau says it is ready for the year 2000, ask it to provide test results demonstrating this. If possible, test the service for yourself. If it is ready for certain services but not for others, you should determine what this means to your business. Decide if there is a "work around" you can implement. If the service bureau

says it will have a year 2000 version in the future, you need to assess what that means to your business. A date late in 1999 may be too risky.

- **Financial institutions** (not a part of the SBA information)—You will want to follow the same procedure above for any banks, credit unions, lending institutions, investment firms, or other financial institutions where you do business or have accounts. You want to be absolutely certain that not only will they be able to accurately process your business come January 1, 2000, but that they will be able to maintain a proper and accurate record of your accounts. To be on the safe side, you will want to get a hard copy of any financial records or statements late in 1999, and try to avoid any major transactions that might be scheduled to be posted early into the year 2000 until you are assured that the institution's year 2000 conversion is running smoothly.

- **Utilities and services—**If your local utility fails to provide you with water, gas, or electricity, your buildings will not be usable and your business will suffer. [You not only need to be assured of the utility's year 2000 compliance, but you need to know what their contingency plans are in case of a failure to deliver]. You should also contact other companies that provide essential services such as janitorial, repair, delivery, etc. You should contact all of your suppliers to discuss the state of their year 2000 readiness and make contingency plans.

- **Record storage/retention firms—**You may use such a firm to store critical legal documents and backup tapes off-site. These firms should be contacted to determine their state of readiness. It could be disastrous if you have an emergency and discover that your off-site storage firm can't find your backups.

- **Inventory and supplies** (not a part of the SBA information)—If you run a business that depends heavily on a steady flow of inventory and/or supplies, you may want to stock up toward the fourth quarter of 1999 so that you have enough materials and resources to carry you through the first quarter of the year 2000.

Depending on the type of business you have, you may want to look at alternatives to meeting payroll and other expenditures early into the year 2000, just in case your financial institution is experiencing problems.

- **Emergency services** (not a part of the SBA information)—While certain emergency services are important to most businesses, if you operate a business that is more prone to emergency situations, you will want to be assured that your local emergency and health care facilities are ready for the year 2000. This includes local law enforcement, fire department, emergency vehicle services, hospitals, etc.

- **Telecommunications and transportation** (not a part of the SBA information)—Virtually all businesses live and breathe through telecommunication systems. Make sure your phone systems are ready, as well as your local and long distance carriers, and any other special telecommunication services you count on. If your business is highly dependent on transportation—whether public transportation for employees, delivery of materials or supplies, or shipping of your products—you will want to make sure that there will not be any significant interruptions that will affect your business after New Year's Day 2000.

- **Sanitation services** (not a part of the SBA information)—Whether it is ordinary trash pickup or special waste removal due to the nature of your business, you will want to make contact with your local providers to make sure their services will continue uninterrupted in the year 2000.

There may be other areas of concern that are unique to your business. The key is not to delay but get the ball rolling immediately to check out each critical area that the success of your business relies on to meet demand and deadlines. The more you stay on top of the year 2000 problem and resolve it for your business, the more competitive you can be entering into the new millennium. It just may be that some of your competitors that did not take such preparation seriously will languish or fail in the year 2000.

21

Keeping The Gates Open

Keep your head in all situations . . .
(2 Timothy 4:5)

By now you should be getting a clear picture that your very lifestyle, and that of the majority of world citizens is in serious jeopardy. In the United States in particular, we have wined and dined on a raging bull market that seems to know no end—yet. On the basis of full employment, new found paper wealth, and buoyed optimism, we have spent tomorrow's paycheck on meaningless, frivolous pleasures—much of which have little intrinsic or only depreciating value. Or, maybe like many hard-working people around the world, you are just struggling to stay ahead and provide the basics for your family.

One of the biggest projected threats to the U.S. economy as a result of the Y2K problem is job loss—through layoffs, permanent terminations, or through businesses that have to shut down or go out of business. The prospects and reality of a job loss for most people, at this time, would be financially devastating. While the net wealth of Americans has soared to over $35 trillion in 1998—about four times the U.S. economy—according to *Investor's Business Daily*, June 9, 1998, the financial liquidity of U.S. households would not see the majority of U.S. citizens through 30 days of unemployment.

On the Job Activism

If you fall into this majority category, to survive a period of unemployment, you must plan now. First, you must assume that with most government agencies way behind on Year 2000 fixes, it is possible that any unemployment benefits after December 31, 1999, could be delayed or not forth-coming in a timely manner—or in worst case scenario, not there at all.

The best solution, of course, would not to be out of a job to start the year 2000. To lessen that possibility it is imperative that you check on your employer's progress on becoming Year 2000 compliant. Before you approach your boss or those responsible for your employer's Y2K project, make sure you have a good grasp of the problem and the various ways it could affect your employer's business or service. That way you can ask intelligent but probing questions, and demonstrate your knowledge of the subject. Many employers, particularly small company employers, are not well versed on the Year 2000 and how it will affect them and their business.

Once you have assessed your employer's stage of readiness, offer to help in any way possible—serve on fact-finding or other committees, offer to put in extra time to work on various aspects of the problem, help to get task forces going to better facilitate your employer and fellow employees prepare for the year 2000. There may be numerous other ways you can help that are specific to your employer's needs. Be bold in your offer and suggestions. Encourage all of your co-workers to chip in and help with preparedness issues. This is not a time to be timid. Your employer's business and your income are at stake.

If you work for a government agency or nonprofit organization, do not assume that your job is safe. Every entity and segment of our economy and country will be impacted by the Year 2000 Bug. Remember, some of the nation's key government agencies are the furthest behind on becoming Y2K compliant. You should offer to help in any way possible, as well as be a part of task forces to help facilitate the government's compliance efforts and seek to become informed on each agency's progress. Not only your job is dependent on the government's success, but the stability and welfare of the entire country. So be pro-active in your efforts and stay informed.

Hone Your Skills

If any one of a number of severe economic scenarios develop, the more diversified your skills the better you will be able to survive financially. Increasing your know-how and skill in areas you might consider to be hobbies or diversions, such as mechanical or wood working talent, could go a long way to providing supplemental income or used in bartering for other services and vital supplies. While the time is short, anything you can do to enhance your value and marketability can only be of benefit to you now and in the long term.

Changing Priorities

One of the biggest parts of improving your income flow is decreasing your outgo (see chapter 22 for more details). Assuming you decide to start accumulating needed survival supplies, you may need to clear out some clutter to improve your storage capabilities. Now is the time to get rid of all the things that take up too much time, space, or money, but that you rarely use, or could do without. Your focus should be on prudent and practical survival methods and supplies. If you have been a high spender, but low saver, now is the time to accumulate as much cash as possible—not investments, but liquid cash reserves. If your current budget does not allow for that, then take a critical look at how you can increase your cash position.

Here are some ways you may want to consider to increase your cash position.

1. Convert riskier investments to money market funds, short term treasuries, or short term certificates of deposit (make sure the maturity does not go past December 31, 1999). Remember, if you have benefited from the bull market of the last few years, selling off your equities or equity funds will likely trigger capital gains that will be taxable if they are not in a tax advantaged account. But paying taxes on gains may be preferable to losing assets in a market meltdown.

2. Sell depreciating assets that you rarely use or that are costly to maintain. These could include extra vehicles or expensive trucks and motor homes (unless you plan on using the motor home or other camping unit for Y2K survival), boats not included in any Y2K plans, and other expensive adult "toys." If you have a snowmobile or motorcycle, you may want to keep these as potentially necessary survival transportation. If you have real expensive models, however, maybe a less costly one would function just as well.

3. Sell that time-share, unnecessary, second home or condo and get more liquid by putting any equity build-up in cash.

4. If you have been thinking about selling your small business, now may be the time to accelerate your time schedule. Particularly since good businesses are selling at high valuations, and there seems to be plenty of capital available for people to make you a generous offer.

5. If you have the option of an early retirement with a bonus incentive, you may want to take it if your financial position is such that you can handle an early departure.

6. Find ways to earn part-time income that you will commit to saving 100 percent of your after-tax paycheck.

7. If you have a non-working, able-bodied spouse that does not need to stay home with the children, a short term employment stint could help the family finances. With low unemployment still persistent in mid-1998, many employers are begging for reliable employees. If you have any computer skills whatsoever, you can almost name your price and work schedule.

8. Once you have a considerable cash hoard (at least 3-6 months of living expenses), then focus on reducing your debt load. Particularly anything that encumbers your principle residence, such as a home equity loan. If you have such a loan and credit card debt, too, but can not afford to tackle everything at the same time, then concentrate on the home equity loan and make minimal payments on your credit cards. It you make payments ahead make sure you clearly state that it is to make *advanced monthly payments* and not to reduce your principal. Also, make sure you get a written confirmation of credit for the number of months you have paid ahead.

9. Increase your home survival skills—sewing, canning, dehydrating food, gardening, etc.—as well as strict budgeting and conservation techniques.

10. Take the time to learn other necessary skills from your neighbors, friends, and church members. Share your skills with others who want to learn them.

Keep in mind, that this Year 2000 problem and its lasting effects are potentially so serious that it warrants your daily attention to detail. The more you are willing to lay aside personal pleasures and wants, the greater the chance of your satisfactory survival and that of your family.

Points to Ponder

How liquid are you? Without a paycheck, could you meet all your monthly obligations for one month, three months, one year? How long? ________________

List five things you could do to increase your liquidity.

1. ____
2. ____
3. ____
4. ____
5. ____

List five things you could sell now to raise cash.

1. ____
2. ____
3. ____
4. ____
5. ____

22

A Penny Saved ...

"For where your treasure is, there your heart will be also."

(Luke 12:34)

Although there is much prudent financial advice for those planning for the long haul, much of it seems somewhat immaterial in the midst of an impending or potential financial crisis that could have worldwide and lasting impact. With predictions of Year 2000 problems causing anything from annoying glitches in bank records or ATM transactions to downright scary monetary collapse and financial market meltdowns, what should a person do? One thing is clear, no one is claiming to have a crystal ball on this one. While some financial advisors are advocating staying the course of long term investing, others are talking complete divestiture from the financial markets and banks in favor of harder assets, like precious metals and valuable coins. Of course, often those recommending such wholesale changes are selling such investments exclusively.

Since the Great Depression there has perhaps never been a better time for many of us to learn how to detach ourselves from the emotions and trappings of unfettered materialism. "*Do not be afraid, little flock,*" Jesus says, "*for your Father has been pleased to give you the kingdom. Sell your possessions and give to the poor. Provide purses for yourselves that will not wear out, a treasure in heaven that will not be exhausted, where no thief comes near and no moth destroys. For where your treasure is, there your heart will be also*" (Luke 12:32-34).

In times of seeming unbridled prosperity and satisfied personal pleasures it is hard for many to conceive of giving up anything, much less divesting themselves of everything. But that is what God requires of us—those who have committed to follow Jesus. Not that God does not want us to have anything material, or to enjoy the goodness that His creation has to offer us, but for us to be so emotionally detached from material things that perish, that we can place true value on His everlasting kingdom. The Year 2000 and all its related problems will offer those that call upon the name of the Lord, as well as others, a real opportunity to give testimony to where their heart truly lies.

As with any other period of time, it would be wise and prudent to pay off as much of your debt as possible, with this critical difference to time-honored wisdom. Do not excessively pay off debt if it prevents you from improving your liquidity and cash position. It might be better to be able to buy food with cash and put up with creditor demands, than to have all your debts paid but no cash for essentials in the midst of a financial whirlwind.

Compounding the Crisis

One of the biggest problems of the Y2K dilemma is its potential for self-fulfilling prophecy. There is no question that the problem is huge and with potentially devastating financial and other impacts. If enough people are told that the markets are going to crash or the banks are going to fold, and that they should get their money out, then guess what? If enough people with enough money follow that advice, the markets crash and banks close their doors. The "Catch 22" here is that we are dealing with more than a potential market correction or a banking holiday. According to most authorities there is a very real threat to our monetary system and that of the whole world.

In a worst-case scenario, which is a total monetary collapse, it probably will not matter what asset you have, it will all become worthless or of little use to you. So let's take a look at other plausible developments and stages of readiness. It is important to note that there is no sure-fire scheme being offered by any investment professional.

Before addressing this issue of asset protection it is necessary to look at other factors that could further compound the impact of Y2K.

First, there is the investment market itself. After an unprecedented bull market run that has contributed to the growth of American household assets to over $35 trillion in 1998, the U.S. market has gotten very high priced and risky. Without any other contributing elements, many investment professionals feel the market is due for a significant correction.

Second, with the fast and furious collapse of the Asian markets, particularly Japan and Hong Kong, the financial tidal wave has yet to hit U.S. shores with full impact—but it will (most likely in late 1998 or in 1999) as we approach the year 2000.

Third, the financial impact of Year 2000 repairs and readiness on corporate bottom lines has yet to be realized. Add to this the potential millions in litigation costs for Y2K failures—estimated at over 400 billion dollars—and it could send many companies onto the heaps of also-rans.

Four, there is the potential for another oil crisis that is looming in the background. On top of this, if oil companies have trouble with oil drilling or deliveries due to Y2K glitches, oil and gas prices could skyrocket, pushing the world's economies even deeper into recession or a depression.

Fifth, in addition to an illiquid federal government, far too many businesses and American households are leveraged to the eyeballs with short and long term debt, and are in no position to handle any financial crisis, much less one of the Y2K magnitude. With such limited liquidity, too many companies and individuals will spiral down the slippery financial slope if the Y2K or an associated monetary crisis lasts more than a month or two. In addition, the Federal Reserve reported that last year there were a record number (1.3 trillion) of personal bankruptcies, with the number expected to go higher this year. If a record number of bankruptcies are occurring during times of prosperity, what will happen when a recession, or worse, happens?

Sixth, remember the financial collapse of Orange County, CA? It was largely due to the county's investment in very high risk investments known as derivatives. There are still trillions of dollars in these highly volatile derivatives around the world, most of them owned by financial institutions and governmental bodies. Under the world's current economic turmoil, a collapse in the derivative market could cause catastrophic consequences.

Keeping Financial Records and Being a Y2K Snoop

If you are not in the habit of keeping good financial records, now is the time. It will be absolutely imperative that you have a strong paper trail, documentation, contracts, insurance policies, your home mortgage, and any other document that clearly depicts your ownership or right to anything of value to you. If you have misplaced or lost an insurance policy, get a copy NOW! Have you paid off a credit card or loan recently? Keep the verification that you did so.

If you decide to make multiple payments on your mortgage, credit cards, loans, utilities, and other such things prior to January 1, 2000, so that you are paid through the first two or three months in the year 2000, be sure to do it early enough so that you can request and receive hard copy documentation before the end of December, 1999. **Caution:** before paying loans, credit cards, and your mortgage ahead of schedule make sure you have a conversation with someone in authority at the financial or lending institution to make sure you will get the proper credit and not get an unexpected request for payment in January, 2000.

In December, 1999, try not to make any financial transactions that will change your account statements. During the first part of this month you will want to request a current account status report for every investment, bank account, loan, etc., that you have. Of course, so may everyone else, so good luck in getting the task done. However, your local investment advisor or banker should be able to print you out a status report on your accounts as you wait. Be sure to store all your important financial records and other valuable documents, such as wills and insurance policies, in a secure, fireproof safe, security box, or safety deposit box at your local bank.

As you are checking on and verifying your financial statements also check on the Y2K readiness of every financial institution you do business with. If you can not be assured that they are going to meet their Y2K deadline, then it is time to look elsewhere for that assurance. Be politely demanding for the information you need to feel comfortable for them to keep your business. After all, it is your safety and security, and that of your family that counts the most.

Cash as King? Maybe for A While

This crisis dictates that no one financial strategy, nor a static investment philosophy is likely to work. In today's highly electronically-dependent financial marketplace, it would not take much of a computer disruption or failure to cause a major domino effect on the world's markets. At the risk of contributing to the self-fulfilling prophecy mentioned earlier, it seems only prudent and good stewardship, that if you are nervous or convinced that your hard earned money is at risk in any investment arena, then you should consider safer alternatives. In the short run (prior to year 2000), cash, quality money market accounts, certificates of deposit (with maturities before December 31, 1999), and short-term U.S. Government Treasuries, would be safer options worth investigating with your financial advisor. But if he or she is not one who believes in the impact of Y2K, then look elsewhere for advice.

Keep in mind, that under a worse case scenario, such as a monetary collapse, none of the above might do you much good. If banks or brokerages can not transact business, or the monetary supply chain breaks down, or the federal government can not back its debt obligations, then all of the above could be worthless. However, it is worth such a risk to keep some cash on hand in a safe, accessible place to pay bills, buy groceries, etc., for two to three months, in case the financial system is in turmoil early in the year 2000.

In addition to protecting your investment assets, another reason for converting to cash—whether in your retirement or other investment accounts—would be to prepare for possible investment opportunities after the Y2K dust settles. Many savvy investors, including the great John Templeton, made fortunes during and after the Great Depression by having the foresight to accumulate cash before the collapse of the market and then bought stock in good companies whose shares had been beaten down to a few dollars or less a share. Similar opportunities may develop in real estate or small businesses.

For the longer term, and for those with stronger stomachs, some financial advisors are recommending precious metals (gold, silver, platinum)—principally the more marketable coins—as possible alternatives for some cash. The assumption is that under an economic crisis precious metals might become more valuable, or at least hold their value during a monetary crisis. However, there are safe storage considerations (you wouldn't want your neighbors, or maybe Uncle Willie to know), as well as the possibility that the government could rule that all such coins or bullion are illegal and cannot be used.

Other longer term alternatives for the protection of some assets for those who believe the crisis will be short-lived or that the government will stay solvent, might be all cash commercial real estate portfolios with high quality tenants and no debt leverage. If you believe the federal government will survive and make good on its debt obligations, and there is no rapid rise in interest rates, then maybe a portion of your asset base should be invested in U.S. Government and Agency debt instruments, such as zero coupon treasury bonds.

A word of caution: municipal bonds in particular, but also municipal bond funds, often considered staid, conservative investments, could give way if too many municipalities are forced to default on their bonds or the underlying project supported by the bond goes kaput as a result of Y2K failures or monetary lock-up.

Your Retirement Accounts

Active retirement accounts, ones to which you are still contributing, like 401(k)s, offer some unique challenges for asset protection. Most 401(k) plans have limited investment options, but do usually offer a money market account, fixed rate account, a GIC (guaranteed insurance contract), or a U.S. Government security account as potential safe havens from market volatility. You could re-align your portfolio according to your risk tolerance. Another option would be to take the maximum loan available on your account and convert it to cash, keeping it in a safe place, and then re-deposit it in your 401(k) after the markets settle down. Cash held in a bank safe deposit box, while it may be inaccessible briefly in a bank shut down, would not be susceptible to risk from a run on the bank.

If you are retired or have changed jobs but have not rolled over your 401(k), or similar retirement account, now might be the time to do it. Chose an option that offers a lot of flexibility, perhaps including the use of precious metals as an investment option.

Other retirement accounts, such as IRAs, SEP-IRAs, SIMPLE plans, etc., should be closely scrutinized for safer investment alternatives. While you should try to avoid any income taxes or penalties for early withdrawal, if the economic climate deteriorates, it would be better to lose some of your funds to taxes and a 10% penalty to move to a safer haven, then see it all go down the tube.

If you are retired and using your retirement plan for current income, you will likely want to adjust your strategy. Not only do you want to reallocate your portfolio to more conservative choices, but you may want to take out enough cash for several months of living expenses in the first part of the year 2000. But make such a withdrawal well in advance of the end of 1999.

Should you continue to invest in your retirement account? That depends somewhat on your investment philosophy and long term goals in light of Year 2000. First, if your retirement plan contribution has necessitated that you cut back on personal savings, and therefore liquidity, you may want to reduce your contribution or stop it for a period so you can accumulate more cash outside the plan. Second, if you believe that the principal reaction to Y2K will be mostly a market decline and a brief interruption in financial transactions, then continued investment during market lows—after you are assured that financial transactions can occur without any problems—could offer you an opportunity to get in on a new ground floor.

The potential crisis that we are facing has never been seen or experienced before, and therefore there is really no precedent to draw upon for wisdom and guidance other than the Lord Jesus Himself. The Great Depression was largely a result of careless abandon of sound financial prudence, but there were still utilities, financial structure, and reasonably sound governmental systems in place. But Y2K has the potential to impact every facet of our life. Therefore any financial decision you make, or desire to make, will take much prayer and the council of many trusted advisors (spiritual, financial, legal, accounting, etc.) before you act. But act you must, and the time is short, so don't delay pursuing your alternatives.

One other consideration that might be important to some taxpayers. If you regularly get back sizable tax refunds every year, but spend the money, you may want to check with an accountant about the advisability of increasing your exemptions. But this should only be done if you are committed to saving that extra money in your paycheck toward your Y2K survival fund.

Points to Ponder

When was the last time you mapped out a financial strategy for your financial future, and what was it?

____

____

Write down the names of five trusted advisors (spiritual, financial, legal, or otherwise).

1. ____________________________________
2. ____________________________________
3. ____________________________________
4. ____________________________________
5. ____________________________________

With the Y2K situation developing fast, list five financial strategies that you feel would be best for you and your family.

1. ____________________________________
2. ____________________________________
3. ____________________________________
4. ____________________________________
5. ____________________________________

23

No Place Like Home

A prudent man sees danger and takes refuge,
but the simple keep going and suffer for it.
(Proverbs 22:3)

AUTHOR'S NOTE: The following information on personal preparedness is provided with the permission of Paloma O'Riley of The Cassandra Project in Louisville, CO and is printed in its entirety (index excluded). Any additional comments by the author of this book are enclosed in brackets. This information is provided with the understanding that is based on worst-case scenario. The belief of the people at The Cassandra Project and this author, is that it is always best to prepare for the worst and hope for the best. While the following information is believed to be extensive, you may want to consider other preparedness issues that are specific to your needs and safety. Please see the **disclaimer** *at the end of this chapter.*

I. Communication

A. Phone. Communication is extremely important, often invaluable—especially in emergencies. If there are phone communication failures, you could be cut-off from emergency medical, police, and fire services. Therefore, prepare as if you will have no communication. See **Emergency Medical and Dental Care** for specific details in **IV.C.**

One way of maintaining some form of contact within your family or the outside world is a CB radio and/or a Family Channel walkie-talkie. [A CB can run off a car cigarette lighter with an adapter and may help you to keep in touch with local law enforcement. Check and see what channels they monitor and do they plan on paying close attention to those channels if there are any problems or civil disturbances.] Of course, you must make sure that none of these will be affected by the Y2K problem. As a backup, you can always use children's walkie-talkies, as they're the most likely to work. However, they are only toys. Don't count on them for any significant use. (And make sure you have adequate batteries! See **Radio** for more details.)

B. Pager. If phones aren't working, it is likely pagers aren't either. We couldn't come up with anything that can be used as a substitute (flares, maybe? Pacifiers?).

C. Television. In the event of general and backup power systems failure, plan for life with no television for a couple of days. If you have young children, this may affect you more than those who don't. Prepare by having plenty of games available, and be willing to play. It may also be a good time to read to them, teach a new craft, etc. Whatever, expect to have to be the sole source of entertainment for yourself and your family.

D. Radio. During any sort of an emergency, information becomes extremely important. Radio is more likely to be available. Make sure you have a portable battery operated AM/FM radio with good reception, and enough battery power to last at least a week of continuous play. How many batteries you'll need will depend on the type of radio you have. Check with the manufacturer or test it yourself. By inserting fresh batteries and leaving it on, you can time how long the radio will operate and purchase batteries accordingly [or simply buy plenty of batteries].

Another alternative is the wind-up radio (e.g., the BayGen "free-play" radio with FM/MW/SW frequencies). Typically, these operate for about 1,000 hours. Of course, without electrical power, there may not be anything to listen to anyway.

If any member of your family will be separated from the rest for more than a couple hours, it is a good idea for them to have a radio also, and carry it with them.

A good publication to check out:

Emergency Radio!
Scanning the News as It Happens
by Norm Schrein, 1995
Index Publishing, $14.95

Available through amazon.com or your local book store.

[You may want to check out the possibility of using battery operated ham radios. **Warning**—You must be licensed with the FCC to use one. There are hand held, battery operated ham radios that can be used to communicate locally during emergencies or with family members. With repeaters that relay ham signals you also communicate between towns and cities in your area. HF frequency, battery operated radios can be used for broader communication. Some ham operators adapt their radios to run off of a car battery that can be easily recharged. For more information, check with Radio City, 2663 County Road I, St. Paul, MN 55122 (612/786-2524), or any similar store, or visit the web site for Ham Radio Outlet at www.hamradio.com or call 1-800/444-0047.]

E. Other. Entertainment systems, Walkmans, VCRs, etc., may or may not be affected—unless the power goes out and they don't run on batteries. Don't rely on these to entertain you. Nothing like having a few simple (non-electronic) instruments around for fun.

II. Financial

(See chapter 22 for additional information.)

A. Automatic Deposits. *The best defense is a good offense.* Don't count on your paycheck, social security, child support, etc., payments to be there. If you live from paycheck to paycheck like many people, you'll be severely hit if the money doesn't post to your account as scheduled.

As difficult as it is, set enough cash aside to support you and your family for 6-8 weeks; cash for food, etc. [Under normal economic conditions, the recommendation by most financial advisors is to have 3-6 months of emergency cash on hand.] Checks may or may not be accepted, nor may credit or debit cards. For more information about cash or barter see section **D. Cash**.

B. Automatic Payments. Don't count on your bills, mortgage, etc. being paid for you. Pay them a least 3-4 months in advance, for a 2 month period, extending into February of 2000. It is extremely important that you get hard copy receipts for your records. The burden of proof—as always—will be on you.

If there are penalties associated with pre- or advance payments, discuss this with your creditor. Ask if they will waive penalty fees even if only for a few months. If they won't, try to work out an agreement of suspending any late fee penalties if automatic payments fail to work. Get any and all agreements in writing. [If you are in a position to pay off a credit card, installment loan, or note, you may want to try negotiating a discounted payment as payment in full. If Y2K causes chaos for financial institutions, they could have a lot to lose. Some may be willing to get some money up front before December 31, 1999, rather than the possibility of none after that date. It's worth a try. A friend mine received an offer in the spring of 1998 from a major credit card company he has an account with, offering to cut 40% off his balance due if he would pay up his balance over the next six months. Do they know something we don't, or what?].

C. Bills. If you pay your bills by cash, check or credit card—pay them at least 3-4 months in advance, for a two month period, extending into February of 2000—or have enough cash available for the same period. Make sure to get hard copy receipts for your records.

D. Cash. Nothing beats hard cold cash in an emergency. Expect prices to go up, especially if there are shortages of any goods like food. Put cash aside (in a safe place—not a bank or other location that you may not be able to access at any time) enough to pay for food, fuel, medical care, emergencies, etc., for 2 months.

How much? Monitor your expenditures for a month, all of them, even the incidental. The easiest way to do this is keep every single receipt (making sure you ask for them!) for everything you buy, and have other members of the family do the same. At the end of the month, tally them. Barring unusual expenses, that will give you a good starting figure.

Expect prices to go up when shortages are involved. Inflation is caused by many things—not the least of which is greed. Make sure you know more than one source to purchase goods, and that they are reliable. However, do expect there to be shortages. Even with enough money it just may not be available to buy.

If you aren't able to put aside as much cash as you like, look into the barter economy. Barter is a common practice in many areas. Read up on barter at your local library and acquire goods or list services you may be able to use as currency.

[See chapter 24 for more details on barter and community currency.]

For more information about bartering, we recommend visiting:

"Les French" (one of the oldest bartering networks) at
http://www.lesfrench.com/html/tutorial.htm

"Trade World" at
http://www.thetradeworld.com:80/flyer4.html

"The Barter Station" provides barter services at no charge at
http://www.solutions-4u.com/barter/aboutbs.htm

Survival Bartering by Duncan Long (Paperback, Published by Loompanics Unlimited, ISBN: 0915179377), retails for about $8.00 is a good starter book.

Barter: Buying and Selling Without Cash. How to Cut the Best Deal. By Jack Marks. [An out-of-print book, but may be in your library or at used book stores. Amazon.com will do an out-of-print book search for you.]

E. Credit Cards. Even if retailers have managed to work out their problems with credit cards using "00" in the expiration date, they still need power, and need to be open and operating and willing to accept them. Expect to need and use cash. Also expect that prices will go up and there may be shortages.

[Try to avoid adding to any credit card debt, tasking out new loans, or make any unnecessary purchases. Your primary goal between now and the end of 1999 should be to accumulate as much cash as you think you will need to adequately survive, as well as the purchase of any necessary items suggested in this chapter. Also, be wary of accepting or using credit cards with dates in the year 2000. You can also expect credit card interest rates to go up on unpaid balances, or exorbitant rates to be charged on all your card balances—its in the fine print of your credit card contract—usually if you miss even one payment.]

F. Debit Cards. Debit cards [will] have the same liabilities as credit cards. Expect to use cash for most purchases.

III. Food and Other Basic Supplies

A. Food.

1. What to do when (Courtesy of FEMA or Federal Emergency Management Agency)

If the Electricity Goes Off ...

FIRST, use perishable food and foods from the refrigerator. THEN use the foods from the freezer. To minimize the number of times you open the freezer door, post a list of freezer contents on it. In a well-filled, well-insulated freezer, foods will usually still have ice crystals in their centers (meaning foods are safe to eat) for at least three days. FINALLY, begin to use non-perishable foods and staples.

2. What you need.

Long-Term Food Supplies (Courtesy of FEMA)

The best approach is to store large amounts of staples along with a variety of canned and dried foods. Bulk quantities of wheat, corn, beans and salt are inexpensive and have nearly unlimited shelf life. If necessary, you could survive for years on small daily amounts of these staples.

Stock the following amounts per person, per month:

Wheat—20 pounds
Powdered Milk (for babies and infants)*—20 pounds
Corn—20 pounds
Iodized Salt—1 pound
Soybeans—10 pounds (edible)
Vitamin C**—15 grams
*Buy in nitrogen-packed cans
**Rotate every two years

Also include:

Ready-to-eat canned meats [including canned tuna and salmon, or dried meats, such as "jerky" and canned stews, ravioli, etc.], fruits and vegetables.

Canned juices, milk, soup (if powdered, store extra water).

Staples—sugar, pepper [and other condiments].

Vitamins

Ready-to-eat cereals and uncooked instant cereals (in metal containers).

Dry, crisp crackers (in metal containers).

Potatoes (fresh—if you can protect from freezing—or dried flakes or "scallops").

Foods for elderly persons or persons on special diets.

Comfort/stress foods—cookies, hard candy, sweetened cereals,

lollipops, instant coffee, tea bags, cocoa, chocolate bars, canned nuts.

High energy foods—peanut butter, jelly, crackers, granola bars, trail mix.

Vegetable oils.

Dried spices (garlic, onion, oregano, chili powder, etc.).

Baking powder and/or yeast.

Dried beans and/or split peas.

Noncarbonated soft drinks.

White rice.

Bouillon products [and dry mixes, such as soups, chili, spaghetti sauce, etc.].

Dry pasta.

3. Ways to Supplement Your Long-Term Stockpile (Courtesy of FEMA)

The above staples offer a limited menu, but you can supplement them with commercially packed air-dried or freeze-dried foods and supermarket goods. Rice, popcorn and varieties of beans are nutritious and long-lasting. The more supplements you include, the more expensive your stockpile will be.

The following is an easy approach to long-term food storage:

1. Buy a supply of the bulk staples listed above.

2. Build up your everyday stock of canned goods until you have a two-week to one-month surplus.

3. Rotate it periodically to maintain a supply of common foods that will not require special preparation, water or cooking.

4. From a sporting or camping equipment store, buy commercially packaged, freeze-dried or air-dried foods. Although costly, this will be your best form of stored meat, so buy accordingly.

4. Storage

No power means no refrigerators or freezers. The best storage is prepackaged food that won't spoil until opened. Cans, boxed food, beans, pasta, etc., will all survive without refrigeration. Survival rations can usually be bought at an Army Surplus store, and camp rations at a camping supply store.

Milk may be purchased in cans, vacuum packed, or in powder form. Powdered eggs can be used in a pinch, though the taste can leave something to be desired. Baby formula is usually canned or powdered. Word of caution—if you do purchase canned perishables, be sure they are sized for use. You won't be able to store opened cans of milk, etc., without risking food poisoning. Another benefit of canned foods is that they don't require cooking, water or special preparation.

Coolers are always an option, however you have to find a steady source of ice. No electricity, no ice maker. However, those that live in cold climates have an advantage. If the temperature outside is consistently below 32 degrees, a Styrofoam cooler outdoors works well for items like margarine, cheese, etc. Just protect it from animals and curious passersby. [If you live where the weather stays below freezing you may have other options as well. If there is snow or ice outside you can use it to pack perishables in large coolers or other containers and keep them in an unheated garage or shed. If you are close to a frozen pond, lake, or stream, chop out ice to pack around perishable foods.]

Store wheat, corn and beans in sealed cans or plastic buckets. Buy powdered milk in nitrogen-packed cans. And leave salt and vitamin C in their original packages.

Storage Tips (Courtesy of FEMA).

1. Keep food in the driest and coolest spot in the house—a dark area if possible.

2. Keep food covered at all times.

3. Open food boxes or cans carefully so that you can close them tightly after each use.

4. Wrap cookies and crackers in plastic bags, and keep them in tight containers.

5. Empty opened packages of sugar, dried fruits and nuts into screw-top jars or air-tight cans to protect them from pests.

6. Inspect all food containers for signs of spoilage before use.

5. Purchase.

Most of us buy our food at supermarkets. If there is a breakdown in the supply chain, we could experience shortages or store closures. The best alternative is — of course — buying what you need ahead of time. Immediately start laying in non perishable basics like, toilet paper, tissue, dry and can goods, etc.

The cheapest way to purchase goods is by case-lot. It is not always easy to find, but talk to the managers of your favorite store, and see if they'll do so. If the local market closes, you may be able to turn to the local barter market. For more information about barter, see **III.D. Cash**. [For bulk food and essentials, you may also want to check out purchasing co-ops. You could also try to organize your church or neighborhood into bulk buying co-ops.]

You might also want to check out these Web sites:

"Emergency Essentials" at
http://www.beprepared.com or call 1-800/999-1863.

"The Survival Center" at
http://survivalcenter.com/foodstor.html or call 1-800/321-2900 for their catalog.

6. Preservation.

For favorite foods such as strawberries, bananas, etc., you might consider purchasing far in advance and dehydrating. Today's dehydrators are simple to use and very effective. Storage can be as simple as zip lock bags or vacuum seal jars. To extend shelf-life, you can store dehydrated foods in your freezer until needed. Rehydration is simply a matter of adding water, or you can eat them as is, or add to your morning cereal, or in your baking.

You can also use your dehydrator or oven to make jerky. Or, if you're more ambitious, you can try canning. However, make sure you follow directions carefully to avoid any contamination or later spoilage. Your local library should have plenty of books available on both methods. [Your local county Extension Service office should also have plenty of resource information on food preservation.]

7. Preparation.

You can always treat emergency situations like a camp out. A propane or kerosene stove works just fine for most stove-top cooking. The only problem is enough fuel, and proper ventilation. Fire danger increases as well. Make sure you have one or more multi-use fire extinguishers always close at hand—small canister, ABC type. Also, never leave an open flame unattended, especially indoors, and most especially when small children are nearby.

An outdoor charcoal or propane grill can do double duty, as well as your fireplace (as long as it is wood burning). You can also heat food with candle warmers, chafing dishes and fondue pots. Canned food can be eaten right out of the can. If you heat it in the can, be sure to open the can [completely] and remove the label first. Also, canned foods won't require cooking, water, or special preparation. You can also heat food with candle warmers, chafing dishes and fondue pots.

Most camping supply stores have quite a wide variety of devices with which you can cook—from solar to old Sterno cans. Check with them for what may be appropriate for your needs. Also, make any purchases well in advance. Prices may go up, and availability may go down as Y2K approaches.

If these staples comprise your entire menu, you must eat all of them together to stay healthy. To avoid serious digestive problems, you'll need to grind the corn and wheat into flour and cook them, as well as boil the beans, before eating. Many health food stores sell hand-cranked grain mills or can tell you where you can get one. Make sure you buy one that can grind corn. If you are caught without a mill, you can grind your grain by filling a large can with whole grain one inch deep, holding the can on the ground between your feet and pounding the grain with a pipe [or other hard, solid rod].

B. Basic Supplies.

You might want to store the following in large covered plastic storage bins until needed.

Supplies

Mess kits, or paper cups, plates, [bowls] and plastic utensils (you don't want to waste drinking water washing dishes!)

Disposable baby bottle liners.

Flashlights and extra batteries.

Nonelectric can opener, utility knife.

Matches (a waterproof container is useful as well).

Aluminum foil (better than dirtying pans).

Plastic storage containers.

Needles, thread.

Medicine dropper.

Shut-off wrench, to turn off household gas and water.

Candles, lamps and lamp oil.

Battery operated smoke alarms.

Plastic sheeting (in case of leaks, etc.).

Duct tape (for repairs, etc.).

Assorted hand tools.

Wash tub and wash board (for your essentials).

A family size tent (if you live in warmer climates) in case you have friends and relatives fleeing south.

At least one wind-up clock.

One or more of the following: gas grill and propane tanks; charcoal grill and charcoal & lighter fluid; camping stove and fuel

Sanitation

Toilet paper, towelettes (especially for babies).

Soap, liquid detergent (antibacterial soap that doesn't use water is available).

Feminine supplies.

Personal hygiene items (especially deodorant!).

Baby needs (diapers, ointments, etc.).

Contact lenses and solution.

Denture needs.

Extra eyeglasses.

Plastic garbage bags, ties, various sizes (for personal sanitation uses, etc.).

Plastic buckets with tight lids (serve as great potties!).

Disinfectant.

Household chlorine bleach.

Room deodorizer (spray or solid. No wall plug-ins!).

Lime for the outhouse or port-a-potty.

Pets

Food (canned and dried).

Chew toys.

Vitamins.

Litter.

Bedding.

IV. Health

A. First Aid.

Put together a basic first aid kit. You can obtain a basic first aid manual from your local American Red Cross chapter. Include the following:

Sterile adhesive bandages in assorted sizes.

2-inch sterile gauze pads (4-6).

4-inch sterile gauze pads (4-6).

Hypo allergenic adhesive tape.

Triangular bandages (3).

2-inch sterile roller bandages (3 rolls).

3-inch sterile roller bandages (3 rolls).

Scissors.

Tweezers.

Needle.

Moistened towelettes.

Antiseptic.

Thermometer.

Tongue blades (2).

Tube of petroleum jelly or other lubricant.

Assorted sizes of safety pins.

Cleansing agent/soap.

Latex gloves (2 pair).

Sunscreen.

Rubbing alcohol.

Muscle pain relief medication/ointment.

Spandex supports, splints, slings.

Vick's jelly.

Peroxide.

Mercurochrome or iodine.

Non-prescription drugs

Aspirin or non-aspirin pain reliever.

Anti-diarrhea medication.

Antacid (for stomach upset).

Syrup of Ipecac (use to induce vomiting if advised by the Poison Control Center).

Laxative.

Activated charcoal (use if advised by the Poison Control Center).

Cold/sinus relief medications.

Baby aspirin or alternative.

Children's cough medicine.

Some good first aid books are:

The American Medical Association Handbook of First Aid & Emergency Care, by Stanley M. Zydio, James A. Hill.

Baby & Child Emergency First-Aid Handbook: Simple Step-By-Step Instructions for the Most Common Childhood Emergencies, by Mitchell J., M.D. Einzig.

The Complete Idiot's Guide to First Aid Basics, by Stephen J. Rosenberg, Karla Dougherty.

B. Regular Medical and Dental Care.

Try to schedule needed exams, tests, etc., with the results returned well before the end of 1999. If your doctor has not paid attention to the Y2K problem, he may misplace your medical records. Get hard copies of your medical file, x-rays, etc. If you require medication regularly, ask if the doctor will give you a prescription in advance.

Try not to schedule any elective surgery just before or just after the turn of the century. Elective meaning surgery not required for treatment of a life or health threatening or sustaining condition.

C. Emergency Medical and Dental Care.

The greatest concern in an emergency is reaching someone who can help. If the phone lines are down, you might be able to reach emergency services by CB. However, even if phones work, there's no guarantee that the machines and equipment emergency personnel use will work, and correctly. That leaves it up to you.

Take an advanced first aid class, CPR, etc. Learn especially how to tell the difference between life threatening or non-life threatening conditions. When in doubt, however, always err on the side of caution.

Ask your doctor and dentist what to do in a variety of situations, such as a knocked-out tooth, fever, broken bones, falls, [choking, seizures] etc. Make sure you have all the medications needed, extra prescriptions filled, etc. Learning how to deal with such situations yourself will reduce the likelihood of panic, and increase the chances of survival for the ill or injured person.

If ambulances can't be contacted, you'll need to transport the person yourself, properly and safely. Make sure you know the location of the nearest emergency facilities, and try to contact them before you go. Check with such places before the turn of the century to see what their contingency plans are in the event ambulance service, emergency personnel, communications, and power fails.

Remember, don't expect the same quality of care you're used to if there is a general emergency in your community. Try to help out, not demand you be treated before others. Some good medical emergency books are:

Emergency Medical Treatment: Infants, Children, and Adults: A Handbook on What to Do in an Emergency to Keep Someone Alive Until Help Arrives, by Stephen N. Vogel, David H. Manhoff.

The American Medical Association Handbook of First Aid & Emergency Care, by Stanley M. Zydio, James A. Hill.

D. Medical Devices.

If you or anyone you know is dependent on medical devices, it is important to contact the manufacturer and get their assurance—

in writing—that the device will function correctly and safely. Also, speak to the Physician and express your concerns about the devices. Ask the Physician what alternatives there are to electronic or electrical medical devices, or what you can do if the device fails for any reason. Education is really your only option in this area.

According to FEMA, anyone requiring any type of life support that uses electricity should register with their local Emergency Management office—regardless of possible circumstances.

Devices that may be affected include:

Infusion pumps in intravenous drips.

Heart defibrillators.

Pacemakers.

Intensive care monitors.

MRI's.

CT and PET scans.

Dialysis.

Chemotherapy and radiation equipment.

Laboratory, radiology and other diagnostic systems.

Monitoring and control systems, including environmental and safety equipment.

[There is considerable disagreement as to whether or not Y2K will have an effect on pacemakers. Those most suspect are older models. Check with your doctor or manufacturer of the device.]

E. Medical Conditions.

The frail elderly, people with particular medical problems that may need a care giver to perform daily tasks, and people with handicaps, must make special plans for their safety in the event Y2K related emergency service failures occur.

Those who have the following conditions may be especially at risk and should take special precautions:

Acute or chronic respirator illnesses.

Heart ailments.
Unstable or juvenile diabetes.
Dependence on tube feeding.
Epilepsy.
Tracheotomies.
Urinary catheters.
Colostomies.
Dialysis - dependence.

F. Pharmacies and Medication.

Your pharmacy maintains its records on computers, as most businesses. They are subject to the same problems. If you take medication regularly, it is a good idea to ask your Doctor to write you an additional prescription ahead of time, to protect you if the pharmacy experiences any problems or delays.

Some problems may be prematurely expired prescriptions, accessing old file information no longer current, changed medication and dosage, etc. They may also lose your information, or have trouble processing it with your insurance carrier. Don't forget to bring cash with you when its time to purchase.

If you are able to receive medication during and immediately after the date change, check your prescription information carefully for your name, drug name, dosage, quantity, expiration, etc. Errors are still possible, and it's a good habit to practice regardless.

V. Power

A. Heat.

In cold climates, lack of heat can be life threatening. The ill, elderly, and small children are particularly susceptible. The same is true of very hot climates. If the power goes off, it is likely that you will not be able to heat your home if you use electric, or electric fired gas or oil. If power does not go off, you may still be vulnerable if your home temperature control system shuts down. Ask the manufacturer of your system if it will function.

If you depend on air conditioners, etc., you face the same problems. A cool, darkened basement may be good refuge during the heat of the day. Also, battery powered fans should help keep the air circulating, making you feel more comfortable if not cooler.

Always drink plenty of water to combat dehydration in hot climates, and dress accordingly. Restrict activity to the cooler parts of the day. Cover the inside of windows with aluminum foil to reflect the heat away from the house, or use blankets or sheets. You can also rig a shelter on the shady side of the house using a large tarp; or rig a tarp to shade the side of the house that the sun strikes [it could be one side in the morning and the other side in the afternoon] to keep interior heat down.

If heat is cut off, your fireplace, wood stove, freestanding kerosene heater, or even cans of Sterno may act as an alternate heat source. Since heat circulation without fans is difficult, restrict yourselves to one or two rooms of the house and shut the doors on the rest. Try not to enter or exit the house from the room of the source of your primary heat. However, do make sure there is adequate ventilation to prevent the build up of carbon monoxide, other gases or smoke. Buy a battery powered carbon monoxide detector.

Pile up mattresses, sleeping bags, thick blankets and pillows across from the heat source, but not too near it. Expect to wear additional clothes indoors, such as sweaters or sweatshirts, and thick socks—even to bed. If you have children, have them sleep together, between you and your spouse, or with the family [warm blooded] pet. Dogs, in particular, are great sources of heat. Also, they are great alarms if there are any problems in the night.

B. Light.

Though not necessary for our physical survival, light is very important to our emotional health and stability. Light sources include candles, hurricane lamps, flashlights, battery powered camping lights, etc. Fireplaces and wood stoves can also make cozy evening light, Don't expect to light a room as you're used to with electric light. It won't hurt your eyes to use subdued lighting, even for an extended period of time.

Make sure any open flame is well away from children, pets, or flammables, and secure from accidental contact. Always keep a fire extinguisher close at hand. For safety, use a flashlight when using the stairs or accessing darkened cabinets or rooms.

If you need light close to children (to change diapers, etc.), battery powered is by far the safest. You might consider giving them their own small flashlights for fun and as a way to make them feel more secure (but have plenty of batteries!).

Whatever light source(s) you use, be sure you have an adequate supply of fuel or batteries. Store them where easily accessible, safe, and away from children and pets.

For information on generators, check, contact your county Extension Service or a local electrician or electrical supply house.

[Generators should only be considered as short term emergency power sources, not as a constant power supply. They are expensive to purchase and run, and would require a considerable stockpile of gasoline, which may pose a safety hazard. They would be most important to run critical at home medical devices or sump pumps if seasonal flooding is a possibility, or in rural areas where fuel storage is not a problem.]

VI. Safety

Safety is best accomplished through prevention. Do everything you can to prevent accidents, injuries and fires in your home. Check for frayed or loose rugs, unnecessary objects on stairs, halls and walkways, protruding objects on walls that may be missed in the dark, to name a few.

A very good reference:

American Red Cross

Individual and Family Disaster Safety Tips

A. In the Home.

1. If you use candles, place them in a safe place away from any flammable material.

2. Be sure all children know the dangers of candles, chafing dishes, potpourri scent pots, the fireplace, wood stove, and space heaters.

3. Never leave children alone near an open flame nor with matches.

4. Keep clutter away from the stove while cooking.

5. If grease catches fire, do not throw water on it. Cover the pan with a lid. Be careful. Moving the pan can cause the fire to spread. Never pour water on grease fires, nor try to beat it out with something like a towel.

6. Always keep an ABC fire extinguisher close at hand.

7. Do not store combustible materials in closed areas or near a heat source.

8. In order to avoid injury, turn pot handles away from the edge of the stove, and never wear loose clothing while cooking.

9. Don't leave cooking food unattended for extended periods of time, since this is the most common cause of cooking related fires.

10. Only burn wood in the fireplace, and small amounts of paper at a time to avoid a chimney fire. [Various types of oak are the preferred wood for burning. Other hardwoods may be okay, but avoid softwood trees. Softwoods will burn quickly, and will crackle and pop, sending wood sparks flying, making them a possible fire hazard. Do not burn resinous woods, like pine, spruce, and fir. Resinous woods produce a lot of tar that will build up in your fireplace or wood stove flue. An alternate source of burnable oak

might be wood pallets that are frequently made out of oak. Check with businesses and companies in your area that normally ship or receive equipment or other heavy items on wood pallets. Be sure to use a fireplace screen to prevent sparks from flying out of the fireplace or wood stove.]

11. Have your chimney cleaned and flue checked before using.

12. Buy a battery operated smoke detector. If you already have one, clean and test it. A working smoke detector can double your chances of survival.

13. Practice home fire drills. Designate two exits from every room, make sure all family members are aware of an outside meeting place, and get out quickly.

14. If your house catches fire, DO NOT ATTEMPT TO PUT IT OUT. Fire spreads faster than you can possibly imagine—a matter of seconds. Evacuate immediately. Contact the local fire department AFTER you have left the building. Even if you can't reach the fire department, do not try to put out the fire yourself.

15. NEVER go back into a burning building to retrieve belongings or pets.

A really good book for kids:

Disaster Blaster: A Kid's Guide to Being Home Alone by Karin Kasdin, Laura Szabo-Cohen

B. Security Systems.

Security systems include CCTV, motion and heat detectors, and pressure pads to name a few. These systems all depend on electricity—whether from the grid or backup power systems. Since backups kick in if the power goes out, make sure your backup system will function. The only way to know is to ask the manufacturer. Don't assume anything, and get it in writing.

If the security system is for your home or office, be prepared to make a physical inspection of the site to ensure security if power fails. It may also possible to hire temporary security personnel. Your local police department is probably the best source of information if you have questions or special needs. Don't forget, however, that in a community emergency, home or office security is not a police priority, so don't expect it.

It is NOT recommended that householders or business people arm themselves, especially if they have minimal or no prior experience with weapons. The risks are potentially greater than the benefits. It takes many hours of professional training to use a weapon safely and correctly.

If valuables are a concern, remove them from your home or business. Bank vaults are still the safest place to keep them. However, use vaults only if you won't need the items for a week or so. Office equipment is usually covered by insurance if stolen; however, don't expect replacements for at least 4-8 weeks, if not longer. [Property and Casualty insurance companies are planning to add riders to their policies before the year 2000, saying that they will not cover any losses as a result of any home or business losses related to the Year 2000 bug.]

If security is still a concern, consider a watch dog or manual alarm devices. The best security, of course, is a well-lit area (assuming you have electricity or a back-up power source), the presence of a number of people, and the possibility of animal protection (dogs, a tape of a barking dog, "Beware of Dog" signs, very large bones and food bowls left where they can be easily seen). In the home, a well-lit fireplace or plenty of lanterns will also enhance your sense of security, as well as let potential intruders know that you are home and vigilant. [This would also be an opportune time to have a professional locksmith check out the security features of your home for improvements. Make sure you secure your garage, shed, or other outbuildings where you might need to store vital supplies.]

C. Electronic Locks.

If electronic locks rely on electricity, it is likely that either they won't open—possibly locking a person in or out—or fail in the safe mode by releasing the lock. If this is the case, then security is in question.

Check to see if there is a manual override; if there is, make sure you have the key or information to use it. If not, you may need to force the door if entry or egress is necessary. Prevention is also an option.

If you feel that it is likely the lock will fail, you can keep the door open or block the locking mechanism from engaging. This may cause an alarm to go off, which will require you to override it before hand, or be prepared to explain it to security or police.

D. Key Cards or Code Locks.

Key cards are likely to suffer the same problems as electronic locks. Locks into which you punch a code, may also fail to operate, depending on whether they are manual or electronic. See the preceding on Electronic Locks for more detail.

VII. Transportation

A. Auto.

Anyone who says software in cars isn't a problem has forgotten the recent General Motors Corp. recall. About 292,860 Pontiacs, Oldsmobiles and Buicks from 1996 and 1997 model years were recalled due to an engine software problem. GM said a faulty engine system sequence can cause a backfire during start-up, possibly resulting in a cracked intake manifold which could erupt in a fire.

Could your car fail to function? Once again, you'll need written assurance from the manufacturer. Even with that, start considering alternate transportation such as bicycles, low-tech motorcycles, low-tech cars, etc. Of course, walking is a healthy alternative. If you live in a rural area, horses and carts might be an option. [For those in areas where snow is likely, snowmobiles, snow shoes, or cross country skies should be considered. If you have the resources you may want to look into a much older model car, that was manufactured before computer chips were used, as back up transportation—assuming there will be gas available. A good bicycle might come in handy, as might a good sled and child's wagon to pull home supplies from nearby stores. Make sure you have a tire pump handy and assorted bike repair tools.]

Another aspect might be the unavailability of fuel. Gas stations may experience a variety of electrical or electronic problems, as well as delays in fuel delivery. Storing gas can be extremely hazardous. We don't recommend it.

B. Public Transportation.

Buses will probably experience the same problems as cars. Especially busses, trolleys, light rail, etc. Alternate transportation would be the same as above.

C. Airplane.

Several airline companies have publicly announced that they may not fly if they are not confident that EVERY aspect of flight control, monitoring, communications, etc., will function correctly at the turn of the century. Don't plan on taking plane trips over the century change, or if you do, leave at least two weeks ahead of time, and plan an extended stay. Florida might be nice! As for alternatives, hang gliding will only get you so far.

D. Train.

The rail industry is already experiencing severe problems due to computer malfunctions, not related to Y2K. Don't expect trains to be anymore likely to run than other public transportation.

Also, beware of rail crossings. It has been reported that some microprocessor-based gate and signaling controls have failed Y2K tests.

E. Traffic Systems.

Many traffic systems are microprocessor controlled. If driving, treat every light as if it were a stop sign—even if it is green. As a pedestrian, distrust crossing lights. Also be very wary of Express Lanes that use gates to control the flow of traffic. Personally, I'd avoid them completely.

VIII. Water

A. What you need.

A normally active person needs to drink at least two quarts of water each day. Hot environments and intense physical activity can double that amount. Children, nursing mothers and ill people will need more.

Store one gallon of water per person per day (two quarts for drinking, two quarts for food preparation/sanitation). [Some discount and wholesale places, such as Sam's, sell bottled spring water in cases at an extremely reasonable rate. At current prices, ten cases of 30 16oz bottles would cost under 60 dollars.

B. Storage and Treatment (Courtesy of FEMA).

Before storing your water, treat it with a preservative, such as chlorine bleach, to prevent the growth of microorganisms. Use liquid bleach that contains 5.25 percent sodium hypochlorite and no soap. Some containers warn, "Not For Personal Use". You can disregard these warnings if the label states sodium hypochlorite is the only active ingredient and if you use only the small quantities in these instructions.

Add four drops of bleach per quart of water (or two scant teaspoons per 10 gallons), and stir. Seal your water containers tightly, label them and store them in a cool, dark place. For additional methods of purification, contact your local Red Cross.

Boiling, however, is the safest method of purifying water. Bring water to a rolling boil for 10 minutes, keeping in mind that some water will evaporate. Let the water cool before drinking. Boiled water will taste better if you put oxygen back into it by pouring it back and forth between two containers. This will also improve the taste of stored water.

You can store your water in thoroughly washed plastic, fiberglass or enamel-lined metal containers. Never use a container that has held toxic substances, because tiny amounts may remain in the container's pores. Sound plastic containers, such as soft drink bottles, are good. You can also purchase food-grade plastic buckets or drums. Avoid using containers that will decompose or break, such as milk cartons or glass bottles.

C. Drinking Water.

Sources.

Two good sources of water are large containers you can purchase at your grocery store, and from your own tap. Since there is some debate of the purity of tap water, make sure you treat it before storing it long-term. [If you live where temperatures stay below freezing much of the time in December and January, you may want to fill several flexible plastic 5 gallon water containers with tap water before the end of December, 1999, and store in a secure place where it will freeze. Be sure to leave enough air space at the top of the container when filling it to allow for the expansion of the ice as it forms. You can then thaw as needed and purify as in the preceding to use for drinking water.]

Hidden Water Sources in [or around] Your Home (Courtesy of FEMA).

If a disaster catches you without a stored supply of clean water, you can use water in your hot water tank, in your plumbing and in ice cubes. As a last resort, you can use water in the reservoir tank of your toilet (not the bowl), but purify it first (see Storage and Treatment).

Water beds hold up to 400 gallons, but some water beds contain toxic chemicals that are not fully removed by many purifiers. If you designate a water bed in your home as an emergency resource, drain it yearly and refill it with fresh water containing two ounces of bleach per 120 gallons. Or, use the water only for toilet flushing.

To use the water in your pipes, let air into the plumbing by turning on the highest (elevation) faucet in your house while draining the water from the lowest one.

To use the water in your hot water tank, be sure the electricity or gas is off, and open the drain at the bottom of the tank. Start the water flowing by turning off the water intake valve and turning on a hot water faucet. Do not turn on the gas or electricity [to the water tank] when the tank is empty. [Before draining the tank, you may want to let it set for a couple of hours or more to let the water inside cool down, thus reducing your risk of getting burned.]

Do you know the location of your incoming water valve? You'll need to shut it off to stop contaminated water from entering your home if you hear reports of broken water or sewage lines. Also, in cold climates, frozen pipes may burst if there is no heat. Shut off the water and drain the pipes if there's a strong possibility of this occurring. [Check with your local plumber for tips on how to winterize your home if you think there is any possibility that you will not be able to prevent plumbing freeze-ups if you lose power and heat.]

D. Waste Water.

Waste water and sewage treatment facilities are highly automated and environmental emissions monitoring and control systems depend on year 2000-vulnerable embedded controls. Malfunctions due to year 2000 problems could lead to polluting releases and emissions that could endanger local residents. One mission critical program where work on year 2000 issues was lagging, according to a recent status report, is the pump station network—a system that monitors stations to keep track of sewage and waste water flows.

Be wary of tap water, and gray water used for outside purposes. Home water testing kits can help you check. The best defense is a store of emergency water.

IX. Sanitation and Refuse

As for solid waste, expect delays in garbage collection, etc. Rodents can be a major health threat where garbage accumulates; so make sure you have enough sturdy, lidded containers to hold refuse produced over a 2 week period.

Be prepared to keep your yard clean if other peoples' refuse finds its way to your yard.

Don't allow garbage to accumulate outside your home. In some rural [and suburban] areas, trash can be a particular attractant for a variety of wildlife—some dangerous. Store paper and other flammables away from any heat sources or open flames until it can be disposed of. See also Sanitation Supplies, III.B.

[Basically all communities in the U.S. require water and electricity to process household sewage. Many counties even require an electrical pump to facilitate processing of septic tank waste in rural areas. Under severe Y2K scenarios, not having convenient toilet facilities in the dead of winter is not a pleasant thought. If you are without water but your local utility is unable to process sewage, adding melted snow to the toilet tank so you can flush, will only add to the problem. Therefore, planning for alternate toilet facilities could be one of the most crucial parts of your Y2K planning strategy.

Some alternatives you may consider, albeit not the most desirable, could include the building of an outhouse if you live in a rural location. Chemical toilets such as used by some campers could provide a short-term alternative, but create a waste disposal problem in residential areas. If you or a neighbor own a camper with toilet facilities, that would be satisfactory assuming you had a plan for disposal. Perhaps an agreement with a nearby farmer who would be willing to dig a pit for disposal. Of course, such disposal would probably violate most county codes in the U.S. Another alternative could be a port-a-potty. However, most communities would probably shun that idea unless they see it as a last ditch solution to a potential major problem. This, of course, would be largely dependent on supply and the port-a-potty company's ability to service the unit.]

X. Miscellaneous

A. Disaster Preparedness Training.

FEMA has Independent Study Courses on disaster preparedness, disaster assistance, etc., for the general public *at no cost*. Special seminars, workshops, and broadcasts are offered also *at no cost*, via satellite as part of FEMA's Emergency Education Network, called EENET. [For more information, visit FEMA's Web site at **www.fema.gov/** or write to them at: FEMA, 500 C Street SW, Washington, D.C. 20472.]

B. Preparing Your Home.

Winterize your house, barn, shed or any other structure that may provide shelter for your family, neighbors, livestock or equipment. Install storm shutters, doors and windows; clear rain gutters; repair roof leaks; and check the structural ability of the roof to sustain unusually heavy weight from the accumulated snow or water, if drains on flat roofs do not work. Keep plywood, plastic sheeting, lumber, sandbags and hand tools on hand and accessible.

C. Prepare Yourself.

If you go outside for any reason, dress for the season and expected conditions: For cold weather, wear several layers of loose-fitting, lightweight, warm clothing rather than one layer of heavy clothing. Outer garments should be tightly woven and water repellent. Mittens are warmer than gloves. Wear a hat. Cover your mouth with a scarf to protect your lungs from extremely cold air. Wear sturdy, waterproof boots in snow or flooding conditions.

[For those in severe winter climates make sure you have plenty of warm clothing and accessories for both indoor and outdoor. Include such items as: down coats or parkas; snowmobile suits; insulated boots; wool or insulated socks; wool or acrylic blankets, and / or quilts; down sleeping bags; feather beds are excellent warm covers; wool-lined leather hunting mittens; ski masks and warm, ear-covering winter hats or hoods; sweat shirts and sweat pants; insulated flannel shirts; insulated or thermal underwear, etc..]

For more information,
contact The Cassandra Project:
address: P. O. Box 8

Louisville, CO 80027-0008
Phone: 303/664-5227
Web Site: **http://millennia-bcs.com/casframe.htm**

Disclaimer. The information in this chapter was mostly provided with permission by The Cassandra Group, and is provided by them and the author as general information in regard to the subject matter being covered. It is provided with the understanding that neither The Cassandra Group, the author of its information, nor the author and publisher of this book is engaged in rendering legal, medical, financial, or other professional services through this publication. It should not be used as a substitute for professional legal, medical, financial, technical advice or services if a professional is required.

24

It's A Community Thing

The entire law is summed up in a single command: "Love your neighbor as yourself."
(Galatians 5:14)

With such an impending disaster, what should you do? More importantly, what should a follower of Jesus Christ do? It is easy to think of self preservation and the welfare of your family first. There is nothing wrong with that. It is as God intended, and as our own emotions and dedications would dictate. God expects us to take responsibility for those that He has entrusted to us. But, after that normal response what should we do? Head for the hills? Many, even responsible Christians, are advocating and doing just that. That is not practical, however, for the vast majority of people, nor does it help resolve the problem.

Yet, if we stay put and prepare for the fallout of Year 2000, but our neighbors are not educated to do so, how safe and comfortable will we be if our neighbors are cold and hungry? The apostle Paul says, *"Therefore each of you must put off falsehood and speak truthfully to his neighbor, for we are all members of one body"* (Ephesians 4:25). As Christians, or as just good neighbors, we have a responsibility to inform and educate our neighbors about the need for Y2K preparation. The better prepared our neighbors are, the more comfortable and safe our homes and the whole neighborhood will be during any Y2K crisis.

The Year 2000 challenge will sorely test whether we are sheep or goats. In Matthew 25, Jesus tells the story of how He will come and will separate the sheep from the goats—*"the sheep on his right and the goats on his left"* (verse 33).

> *"Then the King will say to those on his right, 'Come, you who are blessed by my Father; take your inheritance, the kingdom prepared for you since the creation of the world. For I was hungry and you gave me something to eat, I was thirsty and you gave me something to drink, I was a stranger and you invited me in, I needed clothes and you clothed me, I was sick and you looked after me, I was in prison and you came to visit me.'"*
>
> (Matthew 25: 34-36)

Then Jesus says that the righteous ones on His right will ask, *"when did we do this?"* He answered: "*The King will reply, 'I tell you the truth, whatever you did for one of the least of these brothers of mine, you did for me'"* (verse 25:40).

While Y2K will present many personal challenges for each one of us, perhaps the greatest challenge will be our resolve and commitment to reach out and help our neighbors weather the storm, too. As mentioned in a previous chapter, our individual survival and that of our neighborhoods will depend on how well organized and prepared we are to deal with the ramifications of Y2K.

If you are the most informed or concerned about the Year 2000, then rally your neighbors to an information meeting. If you need some authoritative support, you can order the Christian Broadcasting Network's "700 Club" Y2K video tapes of programs aired on July 10, 1998, (personal preparedness) and August 7, 1998, (church preparedness). Order either tape from Burrelle Transcripts by calling 1-800/777-8398.

Use this book and *The Cassandra Project* information as resources to tell the Y2K story. Then suggest that the neighborhood organize into task forces to survey the needs and resources of the group, and how to best supplement those resources and meet the needs of the whole group. A task force should also be formed—if the community at large has not formed one—to solicit and keep up to date on the compliance efforts of such things as key employers, utilities, medical facilities, law enforcement, transportation, communications, and food supplies.

Make lists of general supplies needed by all and seek to leverage your buying or bartering power as a group. Organize work days to build up the neighborhood wood supply for all those that have wood burning capability as an alternate heat source. Of course, this means we should be willing to share such warmth with those that may not have that alternate heat source. Develop a task force to look into the best and most economical sources of bulk food supplies that can then be divided among the neighborhood. As you go about your preparation, be sure to take special note and care of those in your neighborhood that are less able to prepare: the elderly, the sick, the single mothers, the disabled, etc.

Of His followers, Jesus says, *"From everyone who has been given much, much will be demanded; and from the one who has been entrusted with much, much more will be asked"* (Luke 12:48b). As Christians and members of the Body of Christ, even if we are lacking in material goods, we have all been given a great treasure in the person and testimony of Jesus Christ. If there was ever a time when our neighbors and community need to hear about such a treasure, it is now. For those who have been blessed materially, Jesus says even much more will be required of you. Now is the time to share.

In the sixth chapter of Paul's first letter to Timothy at the church in Ephesus, Paul instructs Timothy to share with the followers in Ephesus that *"godliness with contentment is great gain. For we brought nothing into the world, and we can take nothing out of it. But if we have food and clothing, we will be content with that. People who want to get rich fall into temptation and a trap and into many foolish and harmful desires that plunge men into ruin and destruction. For the love of money is a root of all kinds of evil. Some people. eager for money, have wandered from the faith and pierced themselves with many griefs"* (1 Timothy 6:6-10).

Paul later tells Timothy to *"Command those who are rich in this present world not to be arrogant nor to put their hope in wealth, which is so uncertain, but to put their hope in God, who richly provides us with everything for our enjoyment. Command them to do good, to be rich in good deeds, and to be generous and willing to share"* (1 Timothy 6:17-18).

Yes, for those who have much, much will be required. The Year 2000 and the potential struggle it will mean for millions of God's children will severely test those that have much in the world's goods. God will be watching to see how you respond to the test. Will you be tight-fisted and try to hold on to all that you have? Or will you be willing to share with those that God puts in your midst that will need tangible evidence that God loves them, and that He has sent His servants to give testimony, that indeed, HE LIVES!

In addition to helping your church and neighborhood get organized, it may also be prudent and wise preparation—in case of worse case scenarios becoming reality—to look into establishing a barter system. Interestingly, in the midst of our prosperity, many such bartering systems exist today—on a community-wide or national level. Barter is the old style of sharing goods and services among neighbors and is still the main source of trade in many other countries today. Even without the threat of Y2K, a barter system is a good way to build community relationships and cross over the various socioeconomic barriers that artificially separate us. Check Addenda 2 (Web sites) and 6 (Resources) for additional information on how to set up and use a bartering system.

Another concept along the lines of bartering that is spreading throughout communities in North America and elsewhere in the world, is the idea of creating a local currency. Yes, it is legal for a community to establish its own currency or scrip. One of the forerunners in this concept is the town of Ithaca, NY, and their "Ithaca Hours" scrip. It is the brainchild of city planner, Paul Glover. He sees Ithaca Hours as a vital way of stabilizing Ithaca's economy during the Y2K crisis, since the scrip can only be used in Ithaca with Ithaca merchants or service providers. He is even pushing the city to stockpile fuel, use Ithaca Hours to hire people to super insulate the community's homes, as well as help construct waterless composting toilets and cisterns to catch rooftop water within the city limits. If he is successful, he believes it will help Ithaca weather the Year 2000 storm where other communities may not.

For more information on establishing a local currency, write to: Ithaca Money, Box 6578, Ithaca, NY 14851. Or call 607/272-4330, or visit their web site at **www.lightlink.com/ithacahours** for more details. Glover has a book on the subject: *Hometown Money: How to Enrich Your Community with Local Currency*. A packet of information, which includes the book, is available for $25.

Another valuable source of community preparedness information, including a community preparedness checklist, is Napa Valley, CA. You can access the information through their Web site: **www.y2knapa.com.**

Epilogue

Why Y2K's impact could be worse than what even the experts expect

Like many before me, currently, or to come, I have been known to be wrong or make a fool out of myself—but usually in private or among a small group of loving and understanding friends or family members. In the matter of Year 2000 (or Y2K) there tends to be a spectrum of two extremes on the issue: those few who tend to have a narrow, or uninformed view of the problem, and therefore believe it is no big deal; and those that have studied it intensely and see the potential for cataclysmic consequences. Perhaps the majority of Y2K experts believe the outcome will be somewhere in between the two extremes. What is commonly conceded is that no one knows for sure how this will all play out come January 1, 2000, and January 3, 2000 (the first workday), and the days and months that follow. Also stressing is the fact that even the experts tend only to look at their own small picture of the Year 2000 impact analysis, often overlooking the larger, integrated, view of world economies, or the other impending crises that could only worsen the impact of Y2K.

When I first started this research project with some intensity, my thinking fell into the realm of guarded concern. As I started to pull all the pieces of the puzzle together, my concern turned more to controlled alarm. Now, as I complete this book, I see little hope for optimism on the technology front as government agencies, utilities, and companies fall further behind on Year 2000 deadlines, and a majority of the rest of the world sits idle on the Y2K problem. At the risk of going out on a very long limb, I now believe, as do others who understand the complexity of this problem, that the Y2K problem and other accompanying economic challenges has the **potential** of being a greater worldwide threat to our modern day life than the Great Depression was to the United States.

Why do I believe this? Let's put the Year 2000 problem aside for a minute, and assume it does not exist. In the U.S. we have been riding the exuberance of an unprecedented bull market to the point where, by almost every market measure, the market is bloated with extreme over valuation. The call of prosperity and the longest bull market in U.S. history has led many uninformed investors into the market, and with them many seasoned investors abandoning normal investment safeguards and prudent thinking in their quest for their piece of the wealth pie. Stock market wealth now exceeds our national Gross Domestic Product by 50 percent, way above any previous highs. As this paper wealth has escalated upward, U.S. households have pushed their debt level to record highs and their liquid savings to record lows. Just on this scenario alone, the market is ripe for a considerable sell-off. But then there is Asia. As of mid-1998 we have yet to see the real impact of the Asian economic collapse hit U.S. shores. Ripples have already made it, but the tidal wave will likely hit in the fourth quarter of 1998 or early in 1999. When it does, corporate profits will sink, many investors will lose heart and seek safer havens, and the markets will plummet. I fully expect to see a 30-40 percent drop in the U.S. markets from their mid-1998 highs by the end of 1999.

What will compound this market sell-off will be the rapid withdrawal of foreign market capital as market conditions deteriorate, and as the impact of Y2K becomes increasingly more apparent. By the early part of the year 2000, U.S. and world markets could plunge dramatically, wiping out trillions of dollars in wealth virtually overnight. Exacerbating the problem will be the fact that the world's financial markets depend solely on computers to trade over three trillion in currency every day. If this trading is interrupted or shut down, the economies of the world will come to a grinding halt.

The Great Depression of the 1920s and 1930s was primarily a financial collapse created in a large part by financial negligence. It was desperately hard times in the U.S. and in many countries abroad. But, in the U.S. we still had strong government leadership and organization, utilities still functioned, the phone system was operating, commerce flowed, and the framework of society continued to exist. There were thousands of independent banks and none of the mammoth size of today's world banking systems that are deeply entwined with the world financial markets. The **potential** (and I want to emphasize "potential") of Y2K and accompanying economic circumstances, is that none of these supportive elements of our world that we count on daily may exist, at least for a time.

What can and will modify this potential disaster is how we, our churches, and our communities are prepared to deal with the impending crisis. Government is not going to rely on or call upon the Lord, but we can. Government is not going to organize us for survival, but we can. The human factor in this Y2K equation is huge and will define the outcome neighborhood by neighborhood, church by church, and family by family. You can not afford to stick your head in the sand or ignore this problem as if it did not exist or will not affect you. It does, and it will! But you and your fellow members of the local society in which you live can bring about positive solutions and results for the betterment of all. There is nothing in this world that with God's help and a cooperative human spirit that we can not overcome. If the worst happens, we will survive, if we are prepared spiritually, mentally, emotionally, and in practical ways. If the worst does not happen, and our preparation was in vain, then we had the opportunity to grow closer to God and our neighbor. Not to prepare would be to ignore reality and God's call for us to protect and provide for our families and loved ones.

The biggest part of surviving any crisis is not so much the surviving of it, but how we choose to survive at all. The choices we all make now in dealing with Y2K will determine the quality of life come January 1, 2000, and the years thereafter. May we all make such decisions to the glory of God and for the redemption of life here on earth.

Addendum 1

Here is a quick reference list of those talking about the Year 2000 problem. As you recall them from the book or see further comments from them in the news, you can quickly determine the level of expertise or authority with which they speak. Keep in mind that this is only a partial list. There are far too many Y2K authorities to include them all on a list of this type.

Ackerman, Joel. Executive Director, Rx2000 Solutions Institute.

Allegra, Joe. President, Princeton Softech, a Year 2000 consulting firm.

Arnold, Jon. Chief technology officer, Edison Electric Institute.

Baxter, Rob. Honeywell VP in charge of year 2000 compliance.

Bemer, Robert W. "Bob". President of Bigetsoft in Richardson, TX. Mr. Bemer, at 78, came out of retirement after a

40+ year career as computer programmer and created Vertex 2000, software product to help address Y2K computer problems. Phone: 972/671-5000; Web site: **www.bmrsoftware.com**

Bennett, Sen. Bob (R-Utah). Chairman, Senate subcommittee on the Year 2000 Technology Problem.

Boatman, Elizabeth. City of Chicago's computer chief for the Year 2000 project.

Brogan, Tom. Director of network systems for MacNeal Health Network in Berwyn, IL.

Burkett, Larry. Economist and best selling Christian author.

Burns, Sherry. Director of the CIA's Year 2000 project.

Caesar, Diane. Chief information officer for computers at Englewood Hospital and Medical Center, Englewood, NJ.

Clinton, William. President of the United States.

Coffou, Ann K. Managing Director, Year 2000 Relevance Service, Giga Information Group, Boston, MA.

Cummings, Dr. Ian. Head of the Association of Emergency Physicians.

Curtis, Bill. Military computer programmer; head of the Dept. of Defense's Y2K office.

de Jager, Peter. Canadian computer consultant. One of the first to alert companies and governments to the Year 2000 problem.

Dodaro, Gene. U.S. General Accounting Office.

Dodd, Sen. Christopher (D-Conn.). Vice-chairman of the Senate committee investigating the nation's Year 2000 readiness.

Duggan, Jim. Research director, Year 2000 program, Gartner Group, a computer industry research firm in Stamford, Conn..

Farah, Joseph. Editor of WorldNetDailey.com, an on-line daily publication, and executive director of the Western Journalism Center, an independent group of investigative reporters.

Forbes, Steve. Businessman, Honorary Chairman for Americans for Hope, Growth and Opportunity, 1996 Presidential candidate.

Gent, Michehl. President of the North American Electric Reliability Council (NERC).

Gore, Albert. Vice President of the United States.

Greenspan, Alan. Chairman, Federal Reserve.

Gross, Arthur. Former IRS chief information officer and Year 2000 strategist.

Hackworth, David. Retired Army Colonel and critic of the U.S. military's lack of preparedness.

Hall, David C. Embedded Systems Specialist, CARA Corporation, Oakbrook, IL.

Hock, Steven. President of Triaxsys Research.

Hoecker, James. Chairman, Federal Energy Regulatory Commission.

Horn, Rep. Stephen (R-Calif.). Chairman of the House Subcommittee on Government Management, Information, and Technology.

Hotle, Matt. Research director, Gartner Group, an Arizona-based product development company.

Hyland, Mike. Engineering manager, American Public Power Association.

Ingram, Barry. Senior technology executive, EDS Corporation.

Ito, Wendell. Systems analyst, Hawaiian Electric utility.

Jackson, Shirley. Chairwoman, Nuclear Regulatory Commission.

James, Bill. VP, Grocery Manufacturers of America.

Jeanniot, Pierre. Director General of the International Air Transportation Association.

Jones, Capers. Chairman, Software Productivity Research, Inc. in Burlington, MA and Y2K expert. Phone: 781/273-0140. E-mail: Capers@spr.com

Jones, Craig. Executive VP of the Oklahoma Hospital Association.

Kennard, William E. Chairman, Federal Communications Commission.

Kizer, Kenneth W. Veterans Administration undersecretary for health.

Koskinen, John. Chairman of the President's Council on Year 2000 Conversion.

Kozloff, Philip. Citibank's Credit Policy Committee.

Krause, Fred. Forty-one year veteran of Union Pacific railroad in charge of tracking suppliers' year 2000 plans.

Kudlow, Lawrence. Chief Economist, American Skandia, a worldwide insurance and investment company in Shelton, CT.

Lefkon, Dick. Organizer of Y2K conferences worldwide.

Long, Ray. FAA Y2K chief.

Marcoccio, Lou. Gartner Group.

Martin-Jones, Nigel. Spokesperson for Data Dimensions, a Year 2000 solutions consulting company.

McArthur, Larry. President, Ascent Logic Corp., a company that does Y2K assessments for companies.

Minihan, Lt. Gen. Kenneth. Director, National Security Agency.

Montagnolo, Anthony. Vice president of technology for ECRI, a non-profit private agency that evaluates medical devices for Y2K compliance.

Moore, Thomas. Director of the Heritage Foundation's Military Integrity Project.

Mullineaux, Vincent. Founder and President, Millennia III in Westport, CT. Has testified before the Senate Banking Committee of the potential impact of Year 2000.

North, Gary. Editor of the *Remnant Review*. Maintains a Web site with links to great resources and information on Y2K issues of great importance to individuals and churches.

Olson, Larry. Chief Information Officer, State of Pennsylvania. Pennsylvania is one of the states that is leading the pack on getting Y2K compliant.

Parker, Kevin. Head of Information Technology at Morgan Stanley.

Reddy, Michael. Head of securities industry year 2000 unit at EDS Corporation.

Robida, Sheila. Year 2000 project manager for the Connecticut Hospital Association.

Rosotti, Charles. Commissioner of the Internal Revenue Service.

Saffo, Paul. Futurist, Institute for the Future.

Sansolo, Michael. Senior VP, Food Marketing Institute.

Shelton, Gen. Hugh. Chairman, Joint Chiefs of Staff.

Siebenthal, Charlie. Representative of the Electric Power Research Institute.

Spacone, Dr. Alan. Emergency medicine information service consultant for MacNeal Health Network in Berwyn, IL.

Szygenda, Ralph. Chief Information Officer, General Motors Corp., world's largest corporation.

Tenet, George. Director, CIA

Thompson, Sen. Fred (R-Tenn.). Outspoken Senator on the lack of White House leadership on the Year 2000 dilemma.

Ulrich, William M. Co-founder, Triaxsys Research Group.

Unger, Laura S. Commissioner, Securities Exchange Commission.

Webster, Bruce. Founding member of the Washington, DC, Y2K Group that advises government and business on the Year 2000 problem.

Wermiel, Jared. Spokesperson for the Nuclear Regulatory Commission.

Woloszyn, William. Information systems specialist for Integris Health System in Oklahoma.

Wyss, David A. Standard & Poors DRI chief economist.

Yardeni, Edward. Chief Economist, Deutsche Bank Research, Deutsche Morgan Grenfell.

Zvegintzov, Nicholas. President, Software Management Network, Los Altos, CA.

ADDENDUM 2

The web sites below merely represent the thousands of sites that address the Year 2000 issue. I encourage you to seek out other Web sites that might be helpful to you in understanding or preparing for the year 2000. To help you, key Web sites are in ***bold*** *print and offer a wealth of information on the Year 2000 and how you can prepare your home, business, community, and church.*

Select Year 2000 WEB Sites for Additional Information & Assistance

millennia-bcs.com/casframe.htm (Access to information from the Cassandra Project on Y2K preparedness, community and church action).

millennia-bcs.com/prep.htm#fa (Cassandra Project's direct link to Individual Preparation for Y2K).

pw2.netcom.com/~helliott/00.htm (The so-called "Mother of all Y2K link sites" that contains many links to other sites).

survivalcenter.com/foodstor.html (Web site of "The Survival Center", a bulk supplier of nitrogen-packed, freeze dried, and air dried grains, beans, dry milk, meat, soups, and other food stuffs. Order catalog from the Web site, or by calling 1-800/321-2900).

www.angelfire.com/mn/inforest/grassroots.html (Millennium Salons URL site on community preparedness.)

www.believers.org/y2k.htm (Web site and Y2K resource link of Believers Church in Denver, CO).

www.beprepared.com (Site of "Emergency Essentials", mail order supplier of all sorts of emergency gear and supplies. Catalog can be ordered through the Web or by calling 1-800/999-1863).

www.bmrsoftware.com (Web site for Bob Bemer's Bigetsoft Co., developers of Vertex 2000 software to help businesses get their systems Y2K compliant).

www.bog.frb.fed.us/y2k/ (Y2K page of Board of Governors of the Federal Reserve Bank).

www.cbn.org (Christian Broadcasting Network's Web site for Y2K news and resources, including Y2K books and personal preparedness information by the Cassandra Project and others).

www.cfcministry.org (Christian Financial Concepts / Larry Burkett Web site; plans to post Y2K information).

www.compinfo.co.uk/y2k/manufpos.htm#manufacturers (Information access site for most computer manufacturers on y2k compliance information).

www.compaq.com/year2000/ecg0231297.html (Compaq computer's Web site for Y2K information).

www.corel.com/2000.htm (Web site for Corel, software maker for such software as WordPerfect).

www.dell.com/year2000/products/prodinf.htm (Dell Computer's Web site for Y2K information).

www.euy2k.com (Web site of Rick Cowles, author of *Electric Utilities and Y2K*. A site that updates the progress of utility companies on the Year 2000).

www.fema.gov/ (Web site of the Federal Emergency Management Agency. FEMA provides disaster education and assistance and is a good source of disaster preparedness information).

www.ffiec.gov/y2k/ (Y2K page of the Federal Financial Institutions Examination Council).

www.frbsf.org/fiservices/cdc (Federal Reserve Bank of San Francisco's Y2K page).

www.garynorth.com (Y2k Web site of Gary North, editor of the Remnant Review. This site is a master link to everything and anything about the Year 2000 and how it will impact government, society, and the church).

www.garynorth.com/y2k/results_.cfm/martial_law (Gary North's direct site for information on martial law and Presidential Decision Directive 63, signed by President Clinton on May 22, 1998).

www.gateway.com/corp/support/cs techdocs/y2k/ (Y2k Web site for Gateway computers).

www.gmt-2000.com/gmt-2000/homepage_frameset.html (The link to Greenwich Mean Time's home page with evaluations of PC testers and BIOS chips. Useful for PC evaluation).

www.hamradio.com (Web site of Ham Radio Outlet, worldwide distributor of ham radio supplies, etc.).

www.hp.com/year2000/hwstatus/html (Hewlett Packard y2k Web site).

www.infoworld.com

www.intuit.com/support/year2000.html (Web site for Intuit, makers of QuickBooks and Quicken personal finance software).

www.isquare.com/y2k.htm (The Small Business Advisor Web site).

www.jks.co.uk/y2ki/confer/notices/dtisme01.htm (Link to report "Helping the Small Business Tackle Year 2000").

www.josephproject2000.org (The Joseph Project 2000 is a Christian organization based in Atlanta, GA, that is dedicated to helping Christians, their churches, and communities prepare for the Year 2000).

www.lesfrench.com/html/tutorial.htm (One of the oldest bartering networks).

www.lightlink.com/ithacahours (How to create a legal local currency that can be exchanged for services or pay bills).

www.microsoft.com/smallbiz/edge/yr2000/default.htm (Microsoft's Year 2000 page).

www.rightime.com/default.htm (For testing your PC's BIOS for Y2K compliance).

www.RV-y2k.org (Rouge Valley/Medford, Oregon, community preparedness web site.)

www.rx2000.org (A key provider of training, services, and information for and about the health care industry).

www.sba.gov/y2k (Small Business Administration's site for Y2K preparedness for small business).

www.sec.gov.com (Web site of the Securities and Exchange Commission).

www.sec.gov/edgarhp.htm (Site of the Electronic Data Gathering, Analysis, and Retrieval system, or EDGAR, of the Securities and Exchange Commission to provide access to corporation filing information of publicly traded companies. These corporate filings, by SEC requirement are suppose to include the impact of Year 2000 on the company's earnings).

www.software.ibm.com/year2000/ (IBM's Year 2000 Web page).

www.solutions-4u.com/barter/aboutbs.htm ("The Barter Station" which provides barter services at no charge).

www.stateside.com/y2k.html#AR (Y2K progress updates state by state).

www.surviveY2K.com (Access to a sample of Jim Lord's Year 2000 Survival Newsletter).

www.worldnetdaily.com (Visit editor Joseph Farah's *Between the Lines* column for updates on Y2K and White House documents).

www.y2k.com (legal and management information)

www.y2kjournal.com

www.y2knapa.com (Napa Valley, CA, web site on community preparedness. Provides a good community task force Y2K checklist

www.year2000.com (Peter de Jager's y2k Web site that links to much of the Year 2000 information, including a library of daily updated news).

www.year2000.unt.edu (online conference)

www.yourdon.com/index.htm (Site of Edward Yourdon, co-author of *Time Bomb 2000: What the Year 2000 Computer Crisis Means to You!*).

ADDENDUM 3

SBA Y2K System Assessment and Testing Criteria

(Used with permission).

How do you assess whether or not your computer system is ready for the year 2000, and what criteria you should use for testing it? The Small Business Administration has put together some helpful guidelines that are reprinted here for your information and convenience.

Some questions to help you assess your system's readiness.

1. Can the system perform projections through time? For example, can it calculate interest or payments or make inventory projections?

2. Does the system allow for entering dates? If yes, is the year 2 or 4 digits? What happens if you enter "00" or "01?"

3. Will the system operate differently depending on the day of the week? Will it operate differently at month-end, quarter-end, or year-end?

4. Can the system put things in order by date?

5. Does the system allow you to retrieve things by date?

6. Can the system perform date-based calculations?

7. Does the system have a security feature that includes date checking?

Suggested testing criteria.*

The following list is not all inclusive. You should add others based on your business's needs and ignore those that are not appropriate.

1. **Test** the changed system with dates before the year 2000 to insure that it is working properly.

2. **Test** that the changed system rolls over from 12/31/1999 to 1/1/2000 properly.

3. **Validate** the first business day of the year 2000 (1/1/2000, 1/2/2000 or 1/3/2000 depending on your business needs.

4. **Validate** that the system operates correctly at end-of-month (1/31/2000) and will roll over to 2/1/2000 properly.

5. **Test** that the system rolls over from 2/28/2000 to 2/29/2000 properly; operates correctly on 2/29/2000, and then rolls over and operates properly on 3/1/2000.

6. **Test** 3/31/2000 and 4/1/2000 to show that end-of-quarter processing operates correctly.

7. **Test** 1/7/2000 and 1/10/2000 to insure that the system operates correctly on the first Friday of the new century, and on the Monday after the first Friday.

8. **Validate** year display fields, including data entry.

9. **Validate** the year in reports.

10. **Test** that the system sorts in correct order; **validate** all sort processing.

11. **Validate** correct calculation of dates.

12. **Validate** the correct acceptance of dates from the operating systems.

13. **Validate** calculated resultant values from the dates.

14. **Test** that ages are calculated correctly.

15. **Validate** interest and other time-based financial calculations.

16. **Test** expiration date processing.

17. **Test** historical decision analysis.

18. **Validate** time reporting processing.

19. **Test** workflow/materials requisition and inventory processing.

20. **Verify** that billing calculations are correct.

21. **Validate** cycle processing, including day-of-week and/or first business day of the month.

22. **Verify** that the system forecasts correctly.

23. **Test** forward processing—process dates after the year 2000 (2001, 2002, etc.).

24. **Validate** backward processing — process dates prior to 2000.

25. **Verify** historical or archival date processing.

26. **Validate** that the system purges the correct records.

27. **Validate** date and data error handling routines.

28. **Validate** date expansion, if used, both within the application and between interfacing applications.

29. **Validate** windowing, if used, both within the system and between interfacing systems.

30. **Validate** proper handling of special values in dates — 99/99/9999, 88/88/8888, 00/00/000.

31. **Validate** that the system works with the date 1/1/1999 — first date with "99" in the year field.

32. **Validate** that there are 366 days in the year 2000, and 365 days in the year 2001.

33. **Validate** that 9/9/99 (September 9th, 1999) is handled properly.

(See Addendum 5 for additional dates that might impact your business.)

* You may also want to check your personal computer's BIOS (Basic Input Output System), the basic set of instructions that tells your computer how to start, by logging on to the free Web site, **http://www.rightime.com/default.htm.** This site provides information on testing your PC for Year 2000 compliance.

ADDENDUM 4

SBA Personal Computer Y2K Readiness Check

(Used with permission).

The following steps are suggested to determine if a personal computer will roll over to the year 2000 correctly.

The test presented here requires a bootable DOS floppy diskette. This is a safer method to test your PC's system clock because it leaves the data and programs on your PC's hard disk unaffected. If you boot to your C:\ drive, you may end up loading WindowsÒ and other applications from your startup routine. Using a bootable diskette will ensure the integrity of the data and programs on your PC's hard disks. The test script presented here will check your PC's ability to transition to the year 2000 and recognize it as a leap year.

Do not perform the tests by changing your system's BIOS Setup screen.

Create a bootable test diskette. Insert a blank floppy diskette into the PC's A:\ drive. From a DOS prompt, type

FORMAT A: /S. Or from Windows 3.1 File Manager, click on DISK/FORMAT and check MAKE SYSTEM DISK.

In Windows 95, double-click on your My Computer icon. Highlight Disk A and pull down the File Menu and click on Format. Then check Quick or Full erase and Copy System Files

With the bootable diskette created in Step 1 still in your PC's floppy drive, shut down your system (close Windows) and the power off your PC. Don't just hit the reset button or warmboot (CTRL-ALT-DEL).

Turn the power on your PC, and allow the PC to boot from the diskette.

After bootup, DOS automatically shows the current date. Make sure that the correct date is displayed. Otherwise, you may have to set the correct date on your PC's BIOS.

At the Enter new date (mm-dd-yy) prompt, type 12-31-1999.

After changing the date, the current time will be displayed. At the Enter new time: prompt, type 23:55:00.

Turn the power off on your PC and wait at least 10 minutes. If you don't, DOS will appear to transition correctly to the year 2000. However, once you reboot the PC, it will display the incorrect date if your system's RTC [Real Time Clock] has the flaw described above.

Turn the power back on and wait for the boot process to complete.

Type in DATE at the ready prompt. If Sat 01-01-2000 is displayed, your PC's BIOS passes the test.

At the Enter new date (mm-dd-yy): prompt, type 02-28-2000. This will test your system's ability to recognize the year 2000 as a leap year.

After changing the date, the current time will be displayed. At the Enter new time: prompt, type 23:55:00.

Power off your PC again and wait at least 10 minutes.

Turn the power on the PC. Type in Date at the Ready prompt. If Tue 02-29-2000 is displayed, your PC's BIOS passes the leap year test.

To conclude testing, at the Enter new date (mm-dd-yy): prompt, enter the correct [current] date, e.g., 07-04-1997.

After changing the date, the current time will be displayed. At the Enter new time: prompt, type correct time, e.g., 06:00:00.

Remove the bootable diskette from the floppy and power off your PC.

(**Author's Note:** There have been some reports that Windows (R) 95, as well as other Windows (R) versions have not passed Year 2000 compliance testing. Check Microsoft's Web site at **www.microsoft.com/smallbiz/edge/yr2000/default.htm**).

Addendum 5

Other Important Y2K Dates

(Adopted from the SBA with permission).

Just because your computer successfully rolls over to January 1, 2000, doesn't mean you are home-free. Below are some additional dates that the SBA and others suggest could be a stumbling block for your computer system.

7/1/1999. 46 out of 50 states start their Fiscal Year 2000.

10/1/1999. Start of the Federal Government's Fiscal Year 2000, as well as many corporations.

2/15/2000. W2 forms due.

2/29/2000. Leap year date.

4/15/2000. First tax filing date in 2000.

4/30/2000. First month ending on a weekend.

5/1/2000. Tax withholding report due; unemployment tax due.

9/30/2000. Federal Government's end of fiscal year 2000.

10/10/2000. First '6-digit' date for systems that store the date as MDDYY.

12/31/2000 (Sunday)**.** First year end—check to make sure that the year on your system contained 366 days.

1/1/2001. Test to be sure that the system has been instructed to roll over to 2001.

2/29/2001. Invalid date.

12/31/2001. Second year end—check that the year had 365 days.

ADDENDUM 6

Other Important Resources Relating to the Year 2000

A Survival Guide for the Year 2000 Problem. 1997. Jim Lord & Edward Sapp. J. Marion Publishing.

The Ark Institute. Source of information on persoanl food production and security, as well as a source of non-hybrid vegetable seed. (800/255-1912) www.arkinstitute.com

Back to Basics. 1981. Reader's Digest. Available through your local bookstore.

The Cassandra Project. Helpful resource and preparedness information for individuals and communities. Contact: Paloma O'Riley, The Cassandra Project, PO Box 8, Louisville, CO 80027-0008 (303/664-5227). millennia-bcs.com/casframe.htm

Electric Utilities and Y2K. 1998. Rick Cowles. Self-published.

Extension Service. Check with your local extension service for booklets and materials on topics of self-sufficiency, such as: raising rabbits and chickens; root cellars; food storage; using grains for foods; etc.

Gurney Seed and Nursery. 110 Capital St., Yankton, SD (605/665-1671). A source of some non-hybrid vegatables.

Hometown Money: How to Enrich Your Community with Local Currency. Order from Ithaca Money, Box 6578, Ithaca, NY 14851. (607/272-4330). Cost $25.

Making the Best of Basics: Family Preparedness Handbook. 1997. James Talmadge Stevens. Gold Leaf Press. Available through amazon.com.

Managing 00: Surviving the Year 2000 Computing Crisis. 1997. Peter de Jager and Richard Bergeon. John Wiley & Sons.

Rodale Press. 33 East Emmaus, PA 18098 (610/967-5171). Source of publications on health food and food production.

Rx2000 Solutions Institute. Provides training, services, and information about and for the health care industry on Year 2000 compliance issues. Contact: Joel Ackerman, Exec. Dir., Rx2000 Solutions Institute, 4620 West 77th Street, Suite 245, Edina, MN 55435 (612/835-4478) www.rx2000.org Fax: 612/830-0931 E-mail: info@rx2000.org

Seed to Seed. 1995. Suzanne Ashworth, David Cavagnaro. Seed Saver Publications. (800/255-1912).

Time Bomb 2000: What the Year 2000 Computer Crisis Means to You! 1998. Edward Yourdon & Jennifer Yourdon. Prentiss Hall Computer Books.

The Year 2000 Computer Crisis, An Investor's Survival Guide. 1997. Tony Keyes.

Y2K Videos. Year 2000 preparedness aired on the "700 Club" by the Christian Broadcasting Network on July 10, 1998 (personal preparedness) and August 7, 1998 (church preparedness). Order from Burrelle Transcripts by calling 800/777-8398. Cost: $29.95.

ADDENDUM 7

Archive of Government documents

Presidential Decision Directive #63
'Critical Infrastructure Protection'

THE WHITE HOUSE

Office of the Press Secretary

For Immediate Release May 22, 1998

WHITE PAPER
The Clinton Administration's Policy
on Critical Infrastructure Protection:
Presidential Decision Directive 63
May 22, 1998

This White Paper explains key elements of the Clinton Administration's policy on critical infrastructure protection. It is intended for dissemination to all interested parties in both the private and public sectors. It will also be used in U.S. Government professional education institutions, such as the National Defense University and the National Foreign Affairs Training Center, for course work and exercises on interagency practices and procedures. Wide dissemination of this unclassified White Paper is encouraged by all agencies of the U.S. Government.

I. A Growing Potential Vulnerability

The United States possesses both the world's strongest military and its largest national economy. Those two aspects of our power are mutually reinforcing and dependent. They are also increasingly reliant upon certain critical infrastructures and upon cyber-based information systems.

Critical infrastructures are those physical and cyber-based systems essential to the minimum operations of the economy and government. They include, but are not limited to, telecommunications, energy, banking and finance, transportation, water systems and emergency services, both governmental and private. Many of the nation's critical infrastructures have historically been physically and logically separate systems that had little interdependence. As a result of advances in information technology and the necessity of improved efficiency, however, these infrastructures have become increasingly automated and inter linked. These same advances have created new vulnerabilities to equipment failures, human error, weather and other natural causes, and physical and cyber attacks. Addressing these vulnerabilities will necessarily require flexible, evolutionary approaches that span both the public and private sectors, and protect both domestic and international security.

Because of our military strength, future enemies, whether nations, groups or individuals, may seek to harm us in non-traditional ways including attacks within the United States. Our economy is increasingly reliant upon interdependent and cyber-supported infrastructures and non-traditional attacks on our infrastructure and information systems may be capable of significantly harming both our military power and our economy.

II. President's Intent

It has long been the policy of the United States to assure the continuity and viability of critical infrastructures. President Clinton intends that the United States will take all necessary measures to swiftly eliminate any significant vulnerability to both physical and cyber attacks on our critical infrastructures, including especially our cyber systems.

III. A National Goal

No later than the year 2000, the United States shall have achieved an initial operating capability and no later than five years from the day the President, signed Presidential Decision Directive 63 the United States shall have achieved and shall maintain the ability to protect our nations critical infrastructures from intentional acts that would significantly diminish the abilities of:

> the Federal Government to perform essential national security missions and to ensure the general public health and safety:
>
> state and local governments to maintain order and to deliver minimum essential public services:
>
> the private sector to ensure the orderly functioning of the economy and the delivery

of essential telecommunications, energy, financial and transportation services.

Any interruptions or manipulations of these critical functions must be brief, infrequent, manageable, geographically isolated and minimally detrimental to the welfare of the United States.

IV. A Public-Private Partnership to Reduce Vulnerability

Since the targets of attacks on our critical infrastructure would likely include both facilities in the economy and those in the government, the elimination of our potential vulnerability requires a closely coordinated effort of both the public and the private sector. To succeed, this partnership must be genuine, mutual and cooperative. In seeking to meet our national goal to eliminate the vulnerabilities of our critical infrastructure, therefore, the U.S. government should, to the extent feasible seek to avoid outcomes that increase government regulation or expand unfunded government mandates to the private sector.

For each of the major sectors of our economy that are vulnerable to infrastructure attack, the Federal Government will appoint from a designated Lead Agency a senior officer of that agency as the Sector Liaison Official to work with the private sector. Sector Liaison Officials, after discussions and coordination with private sector entities of their infrastructure sector, will identify a private sector counterpart (Sector Coordinator) to represent their sector. Together these two individuals and the departments and corporations they represent shall contribute to a sectoral National Infrastructure Assurance Plan by:

assessing the vulnerabilities of the sector to cyber or physical attacks;

recommending a plan to eliminate significant vulnerabilities;

proposing a system for identifying and preventing attempted major attacks;

developing a plan for alerting, containing and rebuffing an attack in progress and then, in coordination with FEMA as appropriate, rapidly reconstituting minimum essential capabilities in the aftermath of an attack.

During the preparation of the sectoral plans, the National Coordinator (see section VI), in conjunction with the Lead Agency Sector Liaison Officials and a representative from the National Economic Council, shall ensure their overall coordination and the integration of the various sectoral plans: with a particular focus on interdependencies.

V. Guidelines

In addressing this potential vulnerability and the means of eliminating it, President Clinton wants those involved to be mindful of the following general principles and concerns.

We shall consult with, and seek input from, the Congress on approaches and programs to meet the objectives set forth in this directive.

The protection of our critical infrastructures is necessarily a shared responsibility and partnership between owners, operators and the government. Furthermore, the Federal Government shall encourage international cooperation to help manage this increasingly global problem.

Frequent assessments shall be made of our critical infrastructures' existing reliability, vulnerability and threat environment because, as technology and the nature of the threats to our critical infrastructures will continue to change rapidly, so must our protective measures and responses be rapidly adaptive.

The incentives that the market provides are the first choice for addressing the problem of critical infrastructure protection; regulation will be used only in the face of a material failure of the market to protect the health, safety or well-being of the American people. In such cases, agencies shall identify and assess available alternatives to direct regulation, including providing economic incentives to encourage the desired behavior, or providing information upon which choices can be made by the private sector.

These incentives, along with other actions, shall be designed to help harness the latest technologies, bring about global solutions to international problems, and enable private sector owners and operators to achieve and maintain the maximum feasible security.

The full authorities, capabilities and resources of the government, including law enforcement, regulation, foreign intelligence and defense preparedness shall be available, as appropriate, to ensure that critical infrastructure protection is achieved and maintained.

Care must be taken to respect privacy rights. Consumers and operators must have confidence that information will be handled accurately, confidentially and reliably.

The Federal Government shall, through its research, development and procurement, encourage the introduction of increasingly capable methods of infrastructure protection.

The Federal Government shall serve as a model to the private sector on how infrastructure assurance is best achieved and shall, to the extent feasible, distribute the results of its endeavors.

We must focus on preventative measures as well as threat and crisis management. To that end, private sector owners and operators should be encouraged to provide maximum feasible security for the infrastructures they control and to provide the government necessary information to assist them in that task. In order to engage the private sector fully, it is preferred that participation by owners and operators in a national infrastructure protection system be voluntary.

Close cooperation and coordination with state and local governments and first responders is essential for a robust and flexible infrastructure protection program. All critical infrastructure protection plans and actions shall take into consideration the needs, activities and responsibilities of state and local governments and first responders.

VI. Structure and Organization

The Federal Government will be organized for the purposes of this endeavor around four components (elaborated in Annex A).

Lead Agencies for Sector Liaison: For each infrastructure sector that could be a target for significant cyber or physical attacks, there will be a single U.S. Government department which will serve as the lead agency for liaison. Each Lead Agency will designate one individual of Assistant Secretary rank or higher to be the Sector Liaison Official for that area and to cooperate with the private sector representatives (Sector Coordinators) in addressing problems related to critical infrastructure protection and, in particular, in recommending components of the

National Infrastructure Assurance Plan. Together, the Lead Agency and the private sector counterparts will develop and implement a Vulnerability Awareness and Education Program for their sector.

Lead Agencies for Special Functions: There are, in addition, certain functions related to critical infrastructure protection that must be chiefly performed by the Federal Government (national defense, foreign affairs, intelligence, law enforcement). For each of those special functions, there shall be a Lead Agency which will be responsible for coordinating all of the activities of the United States Government in that area. Each lead agency will appoint a senior officer of Assistant Secretary rank or higher to serve as the Functional Coordinator for that function for the Federal Government.

Interagency Coordination: The Sector Liaison Officials and Functional Coordinators of the Lead Agencies, as well as representatives from other relevant departments and agencies, including the National Economic Council. will meet to coordinate the implementation of this directive under the auspices of a Critical Infrastructure Coordination Group (CICG), chaired by the National Coordinator for Security, Infrastructure Protection and Counter-Terrorism. The National Coordinator will be appointed by and report to the President through the Assistant to the President for National Security Affairs, who shall assure appropriate coordination with the Assistant to the President for Economic Affairs. Agency representatives to the CICG should be at a senior policy level (Assistant Secretary or higher). Where appropriate, the CICG will be assisted by extant policy structures, such as the Security Policy Board, Security Policy Forum and the National Security and Telecommunications and Information System Security Committee.

National Infrastructure Assurance Council: On the recommendation of the Lead Agencies, the National Economic Council and the National Coordinator, the President will appoint a panel of major infrastructure providers and state and local government officials to serve as the National Infrastructure Assurance Council. The President will appoint the Chairman. The National Coordinator will serve as the Council's Executive Director. The National Infrastructure Assurance Council will meet periodically to enhance the partnership of the public and private sectors in protecting our critical infrastructures and will provide reports to the President as appropriate. Senior Federal Government officials will participate in the meetings of the National Infrastructure Assurance Council as appropriate.

VII. Protecting Federal Government Critical Infrastructures

Every department and agency of the Federal Government shall be responsible for protecting its own critical infrastructure especially its cyber-based systems. Every department and agency Chief Information Officer (CIO) shall be responsible for information assurance. Every department and agency shall appoint a Chief Infrastructure Assurance Officer (CIAO) who shall be responsible for the protection of all of the other aspects of that department's critical infrastructure. The CIO may be double-hatted as the CIAO at the discretion of the individual department. These officials shall establish procedures for obtaining expedient and valid authorizations to allow vulnerability assessments to be performed on government computer and physical systems. The Department of Justice shall establish legal guidelines for providing for such authorizations.

No later than 180 days from issuance of this directive, every department and agency shall develop a plan for protecting its own critical infrastructure, including but not limited to its cyber-based systems. The National Coordinator shall be responsible for coordinating analyses required by the departments and agencies of inter-governmental dependencies and the mitigation of those dependencies. The Critical Infrastructure Coordination Group (CICG) shall sponsor an expert review process for those plans. No later than two years from today, those plans shall have been implemented and shall be updated every two years. In meeting this schedule, the Federal Government shall present a model to the private sector on how best to protect critical infrastructure.

VIII. Tasks

Within 180 days, the Principals Committee should submit to the President a schedule for completion of a National Infrastructure

Assurance Plan with milestones for accomplishing the following subordinate and related tasks.

Vulnerability Analyses: For each sector of the economy and each sector of the government that might be a target of infrastructure attack intended to significantly damage the United States, there shall be an initial vulnerability assessment, followed by periodic updates. As appropriate, these assessments shall also include the determination of the minimum essential infrastructure in each sector.

Remedial Plan: Based upon the vulnerability assessment, there shall be a recommended remedial plan. The plan shall identify timelines for implementation, responsibilities and funding.

Warning: A national center to warn of significant infrastructure attacks will be established immediately (see Annex A). As soon thereafter as possible, we will put in place an enhanced system for detecting and analyzing such attacks, with maximum possible participation of the private sector.

Response: A system for responding to a significant infrastructure attack while it is underway, with the goal of isolating and minimizing damage.

Reconstitution: For varying levels of successful infrastructure attacks, we shall have a system to reconstitute minimum required capabilities rapidly.

Education and Awareness: There shall be Vulnerability Awareness and Education Programs within both the government and the private sector to sensitize people regarding the importance of security and to train them in security standards, particularly regarding cyber systems.

Research and Development: Federally-sponsored research and development in support of infrastructure protection shall be coordinated, be subject to multi-year planning, take into account private sector research, and be adequately funded to minimize our vulnerabilities on a rapid but achievable timetable.

Intelligence: The Intelligence Community shall develop and implement a plan for enhancing collection and analysis of the foreign threat to our national infrastructure, to include but not be limited to the foreign cyber/information warfare threat.

International Cooperation: There shall be a plan to expand cooperation on critical infrastructure protection with like-minded and friendly nations, international organizations and multinational corporations.

Legislative and Budgetary Requirements: There shall be an evaluation of the executive branch's legislative authorities and budgetary priorities regarding critical infrastructure, and ameliorative recommendations shall be made to the President as necessary. The evaluations and recommendations, if any, shall be coordinated with the Director of OMB.

The CICG shall also review and schedule the taskings listed in Annex B.

IX. Implementation

In addition to the 180-day report, the National Coordinator, working with the National Economic Council, shall provide an annual report on the implementation of this directive to the President and the heads of departments and agencies, through the Assistant to the President for National Security Affairs. The report should include an updated threat assessment, a status report on achieving the milestones identified for the National Plan and additional policy, legislative and budgetary recommendations The evaluations and recommendations, if any, shall be coordinated with the Director of OMB. In addition, following the establishment of an initial operating capability in the year 2000, the National Coordinator shall conduct a zero-based review.

Annex A: Structure and Organization

Lead Agencies: Clear accountability within the U.S. Government must be designated for specific sectors and functions. The following assignments of responsibility will apply.

Lead Agencies for Sector Liaison:

Commerce	Information and communications
Treasury	Banking and finance
EPA	Water supply
Transportation	Aviation Highways (including trucking and intelligent transportation systems) Mass transit Pipelines Rail Waterborne commerce
Justice/FBI	Emergency law enforcement services
FEMA	Emergency fire service Continuity of government services

HHS	Public health services, including prevention, surveillance, laboratory services and personal health services
Energy	Electric power Oil and gas production and storage

Lead Agencies for Special Functions:

Justice/FBI	Law enforcement and internal security
CIA	Foreign intelligence
State	Foreign affairs
Defense	National defense

In addition, OSTP shall be responsible for coordinating research and development agendas and programs for the government through the National Science and Technology Council. Furthermore, while Commerce is the lead agency for information and communication, the Department of Defense will retain its Executive Agent responsibilities for the National Communications System and support of the President's National Security Telecommunications Advisory Committee.

National Coordinator: The National Coordinator for Security, Infrastructure Protection and Counter-Terrorism shall be responsible for coordinating the implementation of this directive. The National Coordinator will report to the President through the Assistant to the President for National Security Affairs. The National Coordinator will also participate as a full member of Deputies or Principals Committee meetings when they meet to consider infrastructure issues. Although the National Coordinator will not direct Departments and Agencies, he or she will ensure interagency coordination for policy development and implementation, and will review crisis activities concerning infrastructure events with significant foreign involvement. The National Coordinator will provide advice, in the context of the established annual budget process, regarding agency budgets for critical infrastructure protection. The National Coordinator will chair the Critical Infrastructure Coordination Group (CICG), reporting to the Deputies Committee (or, at the call of its chair, the Principals Committee). The Sector Liaison Officials and Special Function Coordinators shall attend the CICG's meetings. Departments and agencies shall each appoint to the CICG a senior official (Assistant Secretary level or higher) who will regularly attend its meetings. The National Security Advisor shall appoint a Senior Director for Infrastructure Protection on the NSC staff.

A National Plan Coordination (NPC) staff will be contributed on a non-reimbursable basis by the departments and agencies, consistent with law. The NPC staff will integrate the various sector plans into a National Infrastructure Assurance Plan and coordinate analyses of the U.S. Government's own dependencies on critical infrastructures. The NPC staff will also help coordinate a national education and awareness program, and legislative and public affairs.

The Defense Department shall continue to serve as Executive Agent for the Commission Transition Office, which will form the basis of the NPC, during the remainder of FY98. Beginning in FY99, the NPC shall be an office of the Commerce Department. The Office of Personnel Management shall provide the necessary assistance in facilitating the NPC's operations. The NPC will terminate at the end of FYOl, unless extended by Presidential directive.

Warning and Information Centers

As part of a national warning and information sharing system, the President immediately authorizes the FBI to expand its current organization to a full scale National Infrastructure Protection Center (NIPC). This organization shall serve as a national critical infrastructure threat assessment, warning, vulnerability, and law enforcement investigation and response entity. During the initial period of six to twelve months, the President also directs the National Coordinator and the Sector Liaison Officials, working together with the Sector Coordinators, the Special Function Coordinators and representatives from the National Economic Council, as appropriate, to consult with owners and operators of the critical infrastructures to encourage the creation of a private sector sharing and analysis center, as described below.

National Infrastructure Protection Center (NIPC): The NIPC will include FBI, USSS, and other investigators experienced in computer crimes and infrastructure protection, as well as representatives detailed from the Department of Defense, the Intelligence Community and Lead Agencies. It will be linked electronically to the rest of the Federal Government, including other warning and operations centers, as well as any private sector sharing and analysis centers. Its mission will include providing timely warnings of intentional threats, comprehensive analyses and law enforcement investigation and response.

All executive departments and agencies shall cooperate with the NIPC and provide such assistance, information and advice that the NIPC may request, to the extent permitted by law. All executive departments shall also share with the NIPC information about threats and warning of attacks and about actual attacks on critical government and private sector infrastructures, to the extent permitted by law. The NIPC will include elements responsible for warning, analysis, computer investigation, coordinating emergency response, training, outreach and development and application of technical tools. In addition, it will establish its own relations directly with others in the private sector and with any information sharing and analysis entity that the private sector may create, such as the Information Sharing and Analysis Center described below.

The NIPC, in conjunction with the information originating agency, will sanitize law enforcement and intelligence information for inclusion into analyses and reports that it will provide, in appropriate form, to relevant federal, state and local agencies; the relevant owners and operators of critical infrastructures; and to any private sector information sharing and analysis entity. Before disseminating national security or other information that originated from the intelligence community, the NIPC will coordinate fully with the intelligence community through existing procedures. Whether as sanitized or unsanitized reports, the NIPC will issue attack warnings or alerts to increases in threat condition to any private sector information sharing and analysis entity and to the owners and operators. These warnings may also include guidance regarding additional protection measures to be taken by owners and operators. Except in extreme emergencies, the NIPC shall coordinate with the National Coordinator before issuing public warnings of imminent attacks by international terrorists, foreign states or other malevolent foreign powers.

The NIPC will provide a national focal point for gathering information on threats to the infrastructures. Additionally, the NIPC will provide the principal means of facilitating and coordinating the Federal Government's response to an incident, mitigating attacks, investigating threats and monitoring reconstitution efforts. Depending on the nature and level of a foreign threat/attack, protocols established between special function agencies (DOJ/DOD/CIA). and the ultimate decision of the President, the NIPC may be placed in a direct support role to either DOD or the Intelligence Community.

Information Sharing and Analysis Center (ISAC): The National Coordinator, working with Sector Coordinators, Sector Liaison

Officials and the National Economic Council, shall consult with owners and operators of the critical infrastructures to strongly encourage the creation of a private sector information sharing and analysis center. The actual design and functions of the center and its relation to the NIPC will be determined by the private sector, in consultation with and with assistance from the Federal Government. Within 180 days of this directive, the National Coordinator, with the assistance of the CICG including the National Economic Council, shall identify possible methods of providing federal assistance to facilitate the startup of an ISAC.

Such a center could serve as the mechanism for gathering, analyzing, appropriately sanitizing end disseminating private sector information to both industry and the NIPC. The center could also gather, analyze and disseminate information from the NIPC for further distribution to the private sector. While crucial to a successful government-industry partnership, this mechanism for sharing important information about vulnerabilities, threats, intrusions and anomalies is not to interfere with direct information exchanges between companies and the government.

As ultimately designed by private sector representatives, the ISAC may emulate particular aspects of such institutions as the Centers for Disease Control and Prevention that have proved highly effective, particularly its extensive interchanges with the private and non-federal sectors. Under such a model, the ISAC would possess a large degree of technical focus and expertise and non-regulatory and non-law enforcement missions. It would establish baseline statistics and patterns on the various infrastructures, become a clearinghouse for information within and among the various sectors, and provide a library for historical data to be used by the private sector and, as deemed appropriate by the ISAC, by the government. Critical to the success of such an institution would be its timeliness, accessibility, coordination, flexibility, utility and acceptability.

Annex B: Additional Taskings

Studies

The National Coordinator shall commission studies on the following subjects:
Liability issues arising from participation by private sector companies in the information sharing process.

Existing legal impediments to information sharing, with an eye to proposals to remove these impediments, including through the drafting of model codes in cooperation with the American Legal Institute.

The necessity of document and information classification and the impact of such classification on useful dissemination, as well as the methods and information systems by which threat and vulnerability information can be shared securely while avoiding disclosure or unacceptable risk of disclosure to those who will misuse it.

The improved protection, including secure dissemination and information handling systems, of industry trade secrets and other confidential business data, law enforcement information and evidentiary material, classified national security information, unclassified material disclosing vulnerabilities of privately owned infrastructures and apparently innocuous information that, in the aggregate, it is unwise to disclose.

The implications of sharing information with foreign entities where such sharing is deemed necessary to the security of United States infrastructures.

The potential benefit to security standards of mandating, subsidizing, or otherwise assisting in the provision of insurance for selected critical infrastructure providers and requiring insurance tie-ins for foreign critical infrastructure providers hoping to do business with the United States.

Public Outreach

In order to foster a climate of enhanced public sensitivity to the problem of infrastructure protection, the following actions shall be taken:

The White House, under the oversight of the National Coordinator, together with the relevant Cabinet agencies shall consider a series of conferences: (1) that will bring together national leaders in the public and private sectors to propose programs to increase the commitment to information security; (2) that convoke academic leaders from engineering, computer science, business and law schools to review the status of education in information security and will identify changes in the curricula and resources necessary to meet the national demand for professionals in this field; (3) on the issues around computer ethics as these relate to the K through 12 and general university populations.

The National Academy of Sciences and the National Academy of Engineering shall consider a round table bringing together federal, state and local officials with industry and academic leaders to develop national strategies for enhancing infrastructure security.

The intelligence community and law enforcement shall expand existing programs for briefing infrastructure owners and operators and senior government officials.

The National Coordinator shall (1) establish a program for infrastructure assurance simulations involving senior public and private officials, the reports of which might be distributed as part of an awareness campaign; and (2) in coordination with the private sector, launch a continuing national awareness campaign, emphasizing improving infrastructure security.

Internal Federal Government Actions

In order for the Federal Government to improve its infrastructure security, these immediate steps shall be taken:

The Department of Commerce, the General Services Administration, and the Department of Defense shall assist federal agencies in the implementation of best practices for information assurance within their individual agencies.

The National Coordinator shall coordinate a review of existing federal, state and local bodies charged with information assurance tasks, and provide recommendations on how these institutions can cooperate most effectively.

All federal agencies shall make clear designations regarding who may authorize access to their computer systems.

The Intelligence Community shall elevate and formalize the priority for enhanced collection and analysis of information on the foreign cyber/information warfare threat to our critical infrastructure.

The Federal Bureau of Investigation, the Secret Service and other appropriate agencies shall: (1) vigorously recruit undergraduate and graduate students with the relevant computer-related technical skills for full-time employment as well as for part-time work with regional computer crime squads; and (2) facilitate the hiring and retention of qualified personnel for technical analysis and investigation involving cyber attacks.

The Department of Transportation, in consultation with the Department of Defense, shall undertake a thorough evaluation of the vulnerability of the national transportation infrastructure that relies on the Global Positioning System. This evaluation shall include sponsoring an independent, integrated assessment of risks to civilian users of GPS-based systems, with a view to basing decisions on the ultimate architecture of the modernized NAS on these evaluations.

The Federal Aviation Administration shall develop and implement a comprehensive National Airspace System Security Program to protect the modernized NAS from information-based and other disruptions and attacks.

GSA shall identify large procurements (such as the new Federal Telecommunications System, FTS 2000) related to infrastructure assurance, study whether the procurement process reflects the importance of infrastructure protection and propose, if necessary, revisions to the overall procurement process to do so.

OMB shall direct federal agencies to include assigned infrastructure assurance functions within their Government Performance and Results Act strategic planning and performance measurement framework.

The NSA, in accordance with its National Manager responsibilities in NSD-42, shall provide assessments encompassing examinations of U.S. Government systems to interception and exploitation; disseminate threat and vulnerability information; establish standards; conduct research and development; and conduct issue security product evaluations.

Assisting the Private Sector

In order to assist the private sector in achieving and maintaining infrastructure security:

The National Coordinator and the National Infrastructure Assurance Council shall propose and develop ways to encourage private industry to perform periodic risk assessments of critical processes, including information and telecommunications systems.

The Department of Commerce and the Department of Defense shall work together, in coordination with the private sector, to offer their expertise to private owners and operators of critical infrastructure to develop security-related best practice standards.

The Department of Justice and Department of the Treasury shall sponsor a comprehensive study compiling demographics of computer crime, comparing state approaches to computer crime and developing ways of deterring and responding to computer crime by juveniles.

Bibliography

Preface

1. *Newsweek*, June 2, 1997. "The Day the World Shuts Down"

Chapter 1

1. *Fortune*, April 27, 1998. "Industry Wakes Up to the Year 2000 Menace"
2. *Newsweek* (ibid).

Chapter 2

1. *Newsweek* (ibid).
2. *Webster's New World Dictionary* (2nd college edition), 1976 The World Publishing Company, Cleveland, Ohio.
3. *The Advocate ONLINE*, Baton Rouge, Louisiana, June 13, 1998. "Computer consultant sees millennium chaos"
4. Vincent Mullineaux, President of Millennia III (testimony before Senate Banking Committee), February 19, 1998. "Time Running Out and Cost Increasing for Year 2000"
5. *U.S. News & World Report*, June 8, 1998. "Year 2000 time bomb"

Chapter 3

1. Vincent Mullineaux (ibid).
2. *Newsweek* (ibid).
3. *Russia Today* (Reuters), June 29, 1998. "Russia Doubts Millennium Bug Can be Fixed by 2000"
4. *U.S. News & World Report* (ibid).
5. *Home Office Computing,* January, 1998. "Millennium Bug Infests the Whole Office"
6. *Fortune* (ibid).
7. *The Advocate ONLINE* (ibid).

Chapter 4

1. Greg Pressin, Staff Writer, June 29, *1998 Kansas City Business Journal.* "Year 2000 approaches: Y2K glitch weaves web of Controversy"
2. *Infoworld*, February 2, 1998. "Once you get by all of the myths about the year 2000, you can focus on fixing it"
3. *Business Week,* March 2, 1998. "ZAP! How the Year 2000 Bug Will Hurt the Economy"
4. *Computerworld*, March 9, 1998. "Y2K Spotlight Falls on Suppliers"
5. *Newsweek* (ibid).
6. David C. Hall, Embedded Systems Specialist, CARA Corp., Oak Brook, Ill. E-mail correspondence to the author, June 2, 1998.
7. *Wall Street Journal*, June 2, 1998. "Many Small Business Owners Shrug at Year 2000 Problem"
8. *Fortune* (ibid).
9. *U.S. News & World Report* (ibid).
10. *Yahoo! News*, AP Headlines, June 12, 1998.
11. *Business Week*, March 30, 1998. "Exterminating the Millennium Bug"
12. *Mercury News Washington Bureau*, June 12, 1998. "Year 2000 prospects chill Congress"

Chapter 5

1. *USA Today* Tech Report, February 26, 1998. "Greenspan warns of year 2000 glitch"
2. *Fortune* (ibid).
3. *Money Matters*, Christian Financial Concepts, July, 1998. "Looking beyond the economic headlines"
4. Vincent Mullineaux (ibid).
5. *Mercury News Washington Bureau* (ibid).
6. Lawrence Kudlow, Chief Economist, American Skandia, Shelton, Conn., June 5, 1998. E-mail correspondence to the author.
7. Lawrence Kudlow, June 9, 1998. E-mail correspondence to the author.
8. Lawrence Kudlow, July 8, 1998. "America the Beautiful: A Midyear Report" Faxed to the author on July 9, 1998.
9. Christian Financial Concepts Inc., May, 1998. "Year 2000 Position Paper"
10. *Business Week*, March 2, 1998 (ibid).
11. *Newsweek* (ibid).
12. *Business Week*, August 12, 1996. "Panic in the Year Zero Zero"
13. *U.S. News & World Report* (ibid).
14. *Advocate ONLINE* (ibid).
15. *InformationWeek*, June 15, 1998. "Securities Firms Pass First 2000 Test—Mock trades dated in 1999, settled in following year"
16. *Yahoo! News,* AP Headlines (ibid).
17. *Computerworld* (ibid).
18. *Steve Forbes Memo* (To: Members of Congress and Business and Conservative Leaders), May 15, 1998. "Clinton-Gore AWOL on Y2K"

Chapter 6

1. *Chicago Tribune*, June 13, 1998. "Utilities' Struggle With Year 2000 Bug Could Leave U.S. In The Dark. Senate warned of Possible Blackouts"
2. *The Advocate ONLINE* (ibid).
3. *Business Week*, March 2, 1998 (ibid).

4. *Mercury News Washington Bureau* (ibid).
5. *Newsweek* (ibid).
6. *U.S. News & World Report* (ibid).
7. *Computerworld* (ibid).
8. *Yahoo! News*. AP Headlines (ibid).

Chapter 7

1. Congressional Quarterly, February 7, 1998. "Clinton Establishes Council To Fix 'Year 2000' Glitch"
2. Rep. Stephen Horn (R-Calif.), Chairman, Subcommittee on Government Management, Information and Technology, July 30, 1996. "US Federal Government Year 2000 Survey"
3. *Newsweek* (ibid).
4. *Steve Forbes Memo* (ibid).
5. *U.S. News & World Report* (ibid).
6. *Mercury News Washington Bureau* (ibid).
7. *InformationWeek*, June 15, 1998. "Feds Fall Farther Behind On Year 2000 Projects—Defense And Transportation Departments Are Among Agencies In Worse Straits"
8. *TIMEcom*, June 15, 1998. "Why The Government's Machines Won't Make It"
9. *Computerworld*, June 15, 1998. "Year 2000 question: Where was Al?"
10. *Business Week*, March 2, 1998 (ibid).
11. *Business Week*, February 23, 1998. "Hey, I Owe 99 Years in Back Taxes"
12. *Investor's Business Daily*, June 5, 1998, page A30. "Beware The Illusory Surplus"
13. *Chicago Tribune*, June 14, 1998. "State Struggles To Beat Clock In Year 2000 Crisis"

Chapter 8

1. *Steve Forbes Memo* (ibid).
2. *InformationWeek*, June 15, 1998. "Feds Fall Farther Behind ..." (ibid).

3. *TIMEcom* (ibid).
4. *USA Today* (ibid).
5. *Newsweek* (ibid).
6. *Russia Today* (ibid).
7. *Investor's Business Daily*, June 10, 1998. *Readiness Gauges Keep Falling.*

Chapter 9

1. Rx2000 Solutions Institute, July, 1998. Frequently Asked Questions.
2. *Washington Post*, July 10, 1998. "Health Coalition Warns of Year 2000 Crisis in Medical Devices"
3. *Chicago Tribune*, May 25, 1998. "Hospitals rush to cure millennium bug"
4. *The Boston Globe Online*, June 14, 1998. "Year 2000 problem could cause life-saving machines to shut down"
5. *The Oklahoman Online*, June 25, 1998. "Area Hospitals Brace For Computer Epidemic"
6. *St. Louis Business Journal*, July 13, 1998. "Health-care providers grapple with Year 2000 issue"

Chapter 10

1. *Solution Works*, June, 1998. "FCC Warns of Year 2000 Telecom Disruptions"
2. *The Advocate ONLINE* (ibid).

Chapter 11

1. *Newsweek* (ibid).
2. *Computerworld* (ibid).
3. *TIMEcom* (ibid).
4. *U.S. News & World Report* (ibid).
5. *InformationWeek*, June 15, 1998. "Feds Fall Farther Behind… (ibid).

Chapter 12

1. *U.S. News & World Report* (ibid).
2. 700 Club, Christian Broadcasting Network, July 10, 1998.
3. Vincent Mullineaux (ibid).
4. *Business Week*, March 2, 1998 (ibid).
5. *Fortune* (ibid).

INDEX

Symbols

401(k) 149

A

abide in Christ 93
account statements 147
advanced monthly payments 141
Ahearne, John 17
Airplane 178
Albert Einstein's definition of insanity 88
American Hospital Association 52
American Medical Association 52
American Nurses Association 52
American Public Power Association 31
American Skandia 23
Americans for Hope, Growth and Opportunity 36
Ameritech Corporation 54
Anderson, Chris 3
answering machines 11
Ascent Logic Corp. 18
Asia 19
Asian markets 145
ask, seek, and knock 115
Assessment 127
asset protection 145
Association of Emergency Physicians 53

AT&T 58
ATM transactions 143
Auto 177
Automatic Deposits 156
automatic drafts 58
Automatic Payments 156

B

BankBoston 25
bartering 139
Basic Supplies 164
Baxter, Rob 18
Bennett, Bob 29, 30
Bills 157
BIOS (Basic Input/Output System) 133
breach-maker 87
breach-repairer 87
Britain 10
Brogan, Tom 54
Burkett, Larry 22
Burns, Sherry 36

C

Caleb-type Christian 96
Capital Market Risk Advisors 12
CARA Corporation 15
Cash 157
cash commercial real estate portfolios 149
Cassandra Project 153, 189
Central Intelligence Agency's (CIA's) 36
certificates of deposit (with maturities before De 148
China 19
Christian Broadcasting Network's "700 Club" Y2K vi 189
church (community) dollars 106
church members 103
church-wide—or encourage a community-wide—barter system 106
church's financial committee or advisors 105
CIA Director 45
Citibank's Credit Policy Committee 23
Civil Defense and Red Cross organizations 122
Clinton, President 3, 4, 33, 38, 48
COBOL 2, 10, 17
coffee makers 7, 11

collapsed economy and monetary system 111
comfort 106
Communication 154
communication (telephone, including cellular, page 117
community of saints in Christ 76
computer-numerically-controlled (CNC) machine tool 17
computerized valves 11
Conectiv 31
confession 81
Connecticut Hospital Association 53
conservation techniques 141
contaminate 132
contingency plans 122
contracts 146
copiers 11
Correction and Testing 130
credit cards 146, 158
Critical Infrastructure Protection 3, 48
Cummings, Ian 53
Curtis, Bill 45
cyber-based information systems 48

D

Data Dimensions 11
Data processing service bureaus 134
date expansion strategy 128
date-sensitive software 29
day-to-day operations 103
de Jager, Peter 3, 6, 7, 11, 18, 25, 30, 69
Debit Cards 158
debt load 141
decoding 2
Department of Agriculture 35
Department of Defense 35, 45, 49, 59
Department of Health and Human Services 35
Department of Transportation 35
depreciating assets 140
derivative market 146
Deutsche Morgan Genfell, Inc. 22, 37
digital cameras 11
digital watches 11
Disaster Preparedness Training 183
diversified your skills 139
diversifying asset bases 105

documentation 146
Dodaro, Gene 36
Dodd, Christopher 30
Dow Jones Industrial Average 26
Drinking Water 180

E

Eastern European 19
ECRI 53
EDS Corp. 24
Electric Power Research Institute 30
Electronic Locks 177
electronic switches 11
elevators 7
embedded chip 117
embedded microchips 29
embedded systems 3, 11
Embedded Systems Specialist 15
Emergency Medical and Dental Care 168
emergency services (police, fire, and ambulance) 117, 122, 136
employer's stage of readiness 138
endowment or trust funds 105
Eurodollar 10, 19
Executive Order 4, 33, 48
Executive Order 13083 48

F

faith 84
Far East 19
Farah, Joseph 48
fasting 84
faxes 11
FBI 49
FCC (Federal Communications Commission) 57
FDA (Food and Drug Administration) 54
Federal Aviation Administration 35
Federal Communications Commission 57
Federal Energy Regulatory Commission 31
Federal Highway Administration 35
federal law enforcement agencies 49
Federal Railroad Administration 35
Federal Reserve Chairman, Alan Greenspan 21
Financial institutions 135

Financial Management Service (FMS) 41
financial services (banking, credit union, investments) 117
First Aid 166
fiscal year 7
fixed rate account 149
Food 117, 159
Forbes, Steve 36, 45
forgiveness 82
Forrester Research 16
fulfillment of prophecy 73

G

gap-maker 87
gap-plugger 87
Gartner Group 11, 14, 22, 36, 71
Gates, Bill 68
General Accounting Office (GAO) 46, 71
General Motors 16
Gent, Michehl 32
GIC (guaranteed insurance contract) 149
Global Command Control System 46
Global Positioning System (GPS) 25, 59
Glover, Paul 191
good sources of water 180
governmental services (city, county, and state) 117
Great Depression 79
Great Flood of the Bible 109
greater reliance on God 76
Greenspan, Alan 21

H

Hackworth, David 47
Hall, David 15
Hawaiian Electric utility company 30
health care providers 51
Health Insurance Portability and Accountability Ac 55
Heat 171
heat 117
Heritage Foundation's new Military Integrity Proje 47
Hidden Water Sources in [or around] Your Home (Cou 181
Hoecker, James 31
home mortgage 146
home survival skills 141

Honeywell 18
Hong Kong 145
Horn, Stephen 4, 33, 34
hospital 122
House Ways and Means subcommittee 39
Howe, Anne 58
HR3116 34
Hyland, Mike 31

I

IATA Director General 63
IBM 3
If the Electricity Goes Off ... 159
illiquid federal government 146
impact on the local church 103
impact to their profitability 70
Implementation 132
improving your income flow 139
India 19, 70
"Information Age" 67
Information Technology Association of America 26, 70
informed preaching and teaching on the Year 2000 104
insurance companies 51
insurance policies 146
integrated testing 7
Integris Health System 54
intelligence agencies 49
intercession 80
International Air Transportation Association 63
Inventory 126, 135
IRAs, SEP-IRAs, SIMPLE plans 149
IRS (Internal Revenue Service) 39
"Ithaca Hours" 191
Ithaca, NY 191
Ito, Wendell 30

J

Jackson, Shirley 31
Japan 10, 19, 145
Jeanniot, Pierre 63
Joint Chiefs of Staff 47
Jones, Capers 14, 25, 69
Jones, Craig 53

K

Kennard, William E. 57
Kennedy administration 48
Key Cards or Code Locks 177
Kizer, Kenneth W. 52, 54
Koskinen, John 38, 63
Kozloff, Philip 23
Kudlow, Lawrence 22

L

lack of financial resources 70
Lack of sanitation 52
law enforcement 122
Light 172
liquid cash reserves 140
loans 146
local government 122
Long, Ray 63
Long-Term Food Supplies (Courtesy of FEMA) 159
Long-Term Stockpile (Courtesy of FEMA) 160

M

machine tools 11
machinery 7
MacNeal Health Network 54
martial law 48, 49, 106, 111
Martin-Jones, Nigel 11
McArthur, Larry 18
measuring instruments 11
Medicaid 51
Medical Conditions 170
Medical Devices 169
medical services 117
Medicare 51
microchips 7, 117
microprocessors 7, 8, 11
Microsoft 68
microwave ovens 11
Millennia III 22, 69
Millennial Christ 98
Millennium Bug 1
minimal government services 111

missions or missionaries 104
money market funds 140
monitors 11
Montagnolo, Anthony 53
Moore, Thomas 47
Morgan Stanley 24
mortgage 146
Moschella, David 38
Mullineaux, Vincent 9, 10, 22, 69
multiple payments 146
municipal bond funds 149

N

narrow cash flows 71
NASA 35
National Academy of Sciences 116
National Association of Securities Dealers 18
National Federation of Independent Business 15
National Infrastructure Protection Center 49
net wealth of Americans 138
North American Electric Reliability Council 32
Nuclear Regulatory Commission 31

O

office equipment 7
Office of Management and Budget (OMB) 36
Oklahoma Hospital Association 53
Olson, Larry 41
On the Job Activism 138
One World Order (Government) 71
option of an early retirement with a bonus incentive 140
O'Riley, Paloma 153

P

Pacemakers 52
Pager 154
Pakistan 70
PanAmSat satellite 58
paper trail 146
pardon 82
Parker, Kevin 24
part-time income 141

paycheck deposits 58
Pentagon 46
personal bankruptcies 146
Personal computers 133
Pessin, Greg 13
Pets 166
Pharmacies and Medication 171
Phone 154
photocopiers 7
place of employment 122
plant machinery 11
plateau-sitter 97
positive result of the Year 2000 dilemma 76
practical survival methods and supplies 139
prayer 80
pre-authorized bank drafts 58
precious metals (gold, silver, platinum) 143, 148
Preparation 163
Preparing Your Home 184
Preservation 163
Presidential Decision Directive #63 48, 106
President's Council on Year 2000 Conversion 63
printers 11
programmers 2
Public Transportation 178
publicly traded companies 13
Purchase 162

Q

quality money market accounts 148
Questions for Various Utility Companies 117

R

Radio 155
recession 146
Record storage/retention firms 135
Reddy, Michael 24
regression testing 133
Regular Medical and Dental Care 168
repair 128
repentance 82
resources of the church 106
restitution 83

retirement accounts 149
retribution 82
riot control plan 122
road department 122
Robida, Sheila 53
Rosotti, Charles 39
Russia 10, 19
Russian State Telecommunications 47
Rx2000 Solutions Institute 52

S

sacrifice 84
safer investment alternatives 149
Safety 173
sanitation (sewer, septic service, waste removal) 117, 122, 136, 165, 182
scanners 11
SEC (Securities Exchange Commission) 18, 116
second home 140
Secret Service 49
Securities Industry Association 25
security precautions 46
Security Systems 175
selling your small business 140
Senate Banking Committee 22, 69
Senate Government Affairs Committee 46
sewage services 52
Sharing of personal resources 106
Shell Oil 31
Shelton, Hugh 47
short and long term debt 146
short term certificates of deposit 140
short term treasuries 140
short-term U.S. Government Treasuries 148
Siebenthal, Charlie 30
Small Business Administration's (SBA's) Y2K Checkl 125
smart phones 11
Social Security 3
Social Security Administration 35, 40
Social Security Trust Fund 40
Software Productivity Research 10, 69
Software Productivity Research Inc. 25
Software Productivity Research, Inc. 14
Solution Works 58
South America 19

Southeast Asia 19
Spacone, Alan 54
spiritual warfare 83
stabilizers 11
stand on the promises of God 84
standardization 10
state and local (county and municipality) government 41
Storage 161
storing your water 180
strict budgeting 141
Styblo, Tanya Beder 12
Subcommittee on Government Management, Information 34
supplemental income 139
support 106
survival supplies 139
Szygenda, Ralph 17

T

target date 69
Telecommunications and transportation 136
Television 154
Tenet, George 45, 46
thanksgiving 84
Thompson, Fred 35
time-share 140
tithe or give offerings and financially support 105
total monetary collapse 145
Tower of Babel 2, 66
Traffic Systems 179
Train 179
transportation (public, but also including snow removal) 117
Triaxsys Research Group 16
Trident missiles 46

U

Ulrich, William 16
U.S. Department of Veterans Affairs 52
U.S. Emergency Alert System 59
U.S. General Accounting Office 36
U.S. Government security account 149
U.S. Treasury Department 41
unemployment 111
Union Pacific Corp. (railroad) 62

Univacs 2
utilities 135, 146

V

VA undersecretary for health 52
valuable coins 143
Vendor-supplied products 134
Veterans Administration 41, 54
vital community services 117
voice-mail systems 11

W

Washington DC Y2K Group 68
waste disposal 52
Waste Water 182
water 117, 179
Webster, Bruce 68
Western Europe 19
White House Council 4
White Paper 48
whole armor of God 80
windowing approach 128
Woloszyn, William 54
World War II 79
worship and praise 84
Wyss, David A. 24

X

no entries

Y

Yardeni, Edward 22, 37
Year 2000 compliance for billing, patient care and 51

Z

no entries

To contact
Jim Gauss
or
The Isaiah Project
FAX 507-455-1549
E-mail: isaiahp@mnic.net

The 21st Century Newsletter

Published by The Isaiah Project

Written and edited by James F. Gauss

If you found *Y2K: Crying Wolf or World Crisis?* to be informative, as well as a valuable resource and encouragement to you, you will want to receive Dr. Gauss's monthly newsletter. It is designed to provide you with the latest updates on Year 2000 issues: progress, preparation, new resources, economic and personal finance issues, gardening tips, spiritual encouragement, and much more. It is a newsletter that will not only help you continue to prepare for the Year 2000, but will continue on into the next century to help you deal with and recover from the aftermath of economic and social turmoil. This is not a newsletter that will try to sell you gold coins, survival gear, or rations, but may be able to tell you what resources are available to meet your needs. Cut down on your Y2K research and preparation time with timely information from a Christian perspective.

To order a one year (12 issue) subscription to **The 21st Century**, complete and mail the order form below with your check for $39 (or what you can reasonably afford) made out and mailed to:

The Isaiah Project
1756 Hemlock Ave.
Owatonna, MN 55060

PLEASE NOTE: To make sure you receive all the information published in the newsletter on Y2K, no matter when you subscribe during 1998 or 1999, you will receive all 12 issues published during 1999 (January - December, 1999) as part of your subscription.

- -

Newsletter Order Form

(Please Print)

Full Name ______________________________

Mailing Address ______________________________

City and State ______________________________

Zip ______________ Phone ______________

E-mail address (optional) ______________________________

Check or Money Order enclosed ______________________________

DR. JAMES F. GAUSS

Dr. Gauss is a skilled lecturer and teacher who has given seminars, workshops, and classes to thousands on varied topics since 1965. He has authored numerous newspaper columns and feature articles, as well as feature articles for consumer, trade, and professional publications. He is the author of *Y2K, Crying Wolf or World Crisis?* - Essential Protection for the Christian Family, published in October 1998 by Bridge-Logos Publishers.

He received his Bachelor of Science degree "With Distinction" from the University of Delaware and his Doctorate of Philosophy three years later in 1968 from Rutgers University. His doctoral research received national recognition as the "Most Outstanding Graduate Student Research" in his field.

A professional horticulturist from 1968 to 1983, Dr. Gauss has been involved full-time in the financial services industry since 1984, assisting people in establishing sound financial principles. He has given numerous seminars on various topics of financial interest and in 1990 established the firm of FAMILY & BUSINESS FINANCIAL, to serve the financial needs of families and small businesses. He is registered with the State of Minnesota as Registered Investment Advisor.

He also serves as an OSJ (Office of Supervisory Jurisdiction) Branch Manager for Linsco/Private Ledger (Member NASD & SPIC) the nation's largest independent Broker/Dealer with over 2500 investment professionals nationwide.

As a member of the Owatonna Press Board of Contributors, he is a frequent contributor to the business section for the Owatonna People's Press, and other area newspapers, writing articles on personal, national, governmental finance, and Year 2000 issues. Dr. Gauss is founder of Financial Freedom Ministries, providing financial seminars for churches, organizations, and groups. In 1992, he had a daily radio program, Freedom From Financial Failure and Folly, on a Minneapolis Christian radio station. In 1998, he founded The Isaiah Project to help disseminate information about the Year 2000 and to help individuals, churches, and communities prepare for the impact of the Year 2000 computer problem.

He serves as an adult Sunday school teacher for his church, teaching biblical principles and discipleship.

As a volunteer, he serves as past President and Chairman of the Board for Steel County, Habitat for Humanity program, an international program that enables the less fortunate to become homeowners. He also serves on the Executive Board and is a member of the Public Relations Committee for the local organization. In July 1994, he served as a volunteer home builder and family partner for the Habitat for Humanity Jimmy Carter Work Project ("Blitz Build") on the Cheyenne River Indian Reservation at Eagle Butte, SD.

Dr. Gauss and his wife, Kathleen, have raised five children and have made their home in Owatonna, MN, since 1984.